C000022523

Ian Rush

My
SCRAPBOOK

Ian Rush

My
SCRAPBOOK

Sport Media
A Trinity Mirror Business

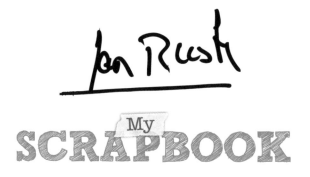

My SCRAPBOOK

Copyright © Ian Rush

Published by Trinity Mirror Sport Media
Executive Editor: Ken Rogers
Senior Editor: Steve Hanrahan
Editor: Paul Dove
Senior Art Editor: Rick Cooke

Senior Writer: Chris McLoughlin
Production: Adam Oldfield
Design: Colin Harrison, Jamie Dunmore

First Edition
Published in hardback in Great Britain in 2013.
Published and produced by: Trinity Mirror Sport Media,
PO Box 48, Old Hall Street, Liverpool L69 3EB.

ISBN: 9781908695109

Photography: Tony Woolliscroft, PA Images, Liverpool Daily Post & Echo,
Mirrorpix, the Ian Rush collection

Printed and bound in Slovenia by arrangement with KINT Ljubljana

To my parents and family,
so many special memories

I think Dad would be proud of My Scrapbook

I'll always remember my dad, Francis, putting together a scrapbook for me when I was a kid.

He'd get the book out regularly, take cuttings from the newspapers and spend time sticking articles and photographs into it.

When I was little, and growing up in Wales, the Evening Leader and the Chester Chronicle would cover schools and youth football. As soon as I started playing, and making a name for myself, Dad would make sure he got those papers so he had a copy of any of the stories in which I got a mention.

As a parent now myself, you feel very proud when your kids get their names in the paper and that's how Dad felt when I was getting a mention for the goals I was scoring.

To be honest, I didn't really take getting my name in the paper seriously back then. I was just playing football because I enjoyed doing it and it just seemed normal, in a way, that the papers reported on local matches.

My dad was one of them who wouldn't show me off. He'd be proud, but wouldn't make a song and dance about me to everyone. I think he most probably kept the scrapbook for himself and for me to look back on when I got older.

When I was playing for Deeside Primary Schools our games would get covered every week, and because I scored nearly every week, I'd end up in the paper a lot.

It's different now. The local papers don't cover junior football to the same level and instead you get reports going on websites.

You've got to move with the times, but the great thing for me is that I'll always have my dad's scrapbook to flick through, look back at the memories and pass on to my kids.

My eldest son, Daniel, plays in the League of Wales, but it was difficult for me to try and keep a scrapbook for him as we were living in the Wirral and couldn't buy a paper that had any stories in about matches he had played in.

We've got pictures of both of my lads playing for their school teams up on the wall but, as I said, you tend to find match reports go on the internet now and printing off a copy isn't quite the same as sticking an old-school newspaper cutting into a book.

Maybe, in the future, things will go full circle and instead of uploading pictures to the internet, parents will want to make their own scrapbooks for their kids. The internet will be old news one day!

My dad, and Cliff Sears at Chester, were the two biggest influences in my career. They were also big mates.

Cliff was great working with kids aged 14-18 and my dad was hugely supportive of me. He didn't drive so he'd take me to Chester on the bus, even taking time off work to get me to games and watch me play. Of course he also kept newspaper cuttings as well!

It is Dad's scrapbook that has inspired me to share the memories of my career with all the fans who have given me such brilliant support over the years.

In 2012, I became the first person to launch a digital scrAppbook. It was quite a step into the unknown for me – nothing like it had ever been produced before for digital devices – but I loved the thought of bringing my medals, shirts, trophies and memories to life in a modern way.

I've had an amazing response to it. I can't believe how many people have seen it and told me how good it was and how much they enjoyed it.

But I'm also aware that not everyone has access to iPads and all that so I wanted to be able to share my memories with all the Liverpool, Chester and Wales supporters who prefer an old-fashioned scrapbook.

Having kept a scrapbook of my career for so many years, I think Dad would've been proud of this scrapbook if he was here today to see it.

Putting it together has brought back some great memories for me – some of the best days of my life – and I hope that as you thumb through the pages, it also sparks some memories of your own.

Memories are precious, something that can never be taken away from you, and I'm both privileged and proud to share mine with you all.

I hope you enjoy my scrapbook and for being the inspiration behind it – thanks, Dad.

Ian Rush

CONTENTS

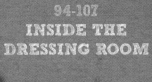

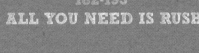

WHERE IT

ALL STARTED

Year Of The Dragon
October 20, 1961

My dad was one of the biggest nationalists you'll ever meet. He was a very proud Welshman. Where we lived in Flint was 12 miles to Chester hospital and 18 miles to St Asaph. I was born in St Asaph, even though it was further away, because there was no way I was going to be born in England!

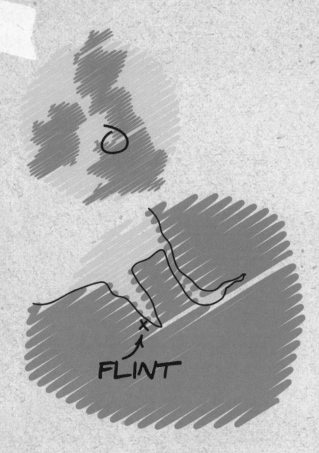

About Flint:

Flint (*Welsh: Y Fflint*) *is a town in Flintshire, North Wales on the estuary of the River Dee.*

It has the oldest town charter in Wales, dating from 1284.

Many people in Flint have some knowledge of the Welsh language, although English is the main spoken language. The Flint accent is most often mistaken for a Liverpool accent. It is, in fact, a unique combination of speech patterns shared with other Welsh speakers, old Irish settlers and those found in nearby Cheshire, Wirral and Merseyside.

There are several songs associated with Flint. The most widely sung is "The Yard". Another popular song is "Fifty German Bombers Over Flint", which tells the story of a wartime bombing raid over nearby Liverpool that accidentally targeted the town of Flint instead.

Other famous footballers who are from Flint include Ron Hewitt, who starred in Wales' only football World Cup appearance, and his nephew, Andy Holden.

Other famous people connected with the town include the chemist John Thomas, best known for his research into plant dyes; and Thomas Totty, an Admiral who served with Lord Nelson and inherited Cornist Hall, Flint. The actor Ian Puleston-Davies also comes from Flint.

Tom Cruise's paternal great-great grandfather, Dylan Henry Mapother, emigrated to Louisville, Kentucky from Flint in 1850.

Jade Jones is Britain's first Olympic taekwondo gold medalist and Youth Olympic champion and lives in Flint. The local sports centre was renamed in her honour following her success at the London 2012 Olympics.

YQ 245888

1 & 2 ELIZ. 2 CH. 20

B. Cert. S.
S.R.

CERTIFICATE
TYSTYSGRIF

OF BIRTH
GENEDIGAETH

Name and Surname Enw a Chyfenw }	Ian James Rush
Sex Rhyw	Boy
Date of Birth Dyddiad y Geni	Twentieth October 1961

Place of Birth	Registration District Dosbarth Cofrestru }	St Asaph
Lle y Ganwyd	Sub-district Is-ddosbarth }	St Asaph

I,
Yr wyf I, } Doris Williams {Superintendant Registrar
Cofrestrydd Arolygol

for the Registration District of }
Dosbarth Cofrestru Rhuddlan

do hereby certify that the above particulars have been compiled from an entry in a register in my custody.

yn tystio yma fod y manylion uchod wedi eu casglu o gofnod mewn cofrestr a gedwir gennyf i.

Date **23 . 4 . 80**
Dyddiad

D. Williams
Superintendent Registrar
Cofrestrydd Arolygol

M20P 271

My first scrapbook and some of the local newspaper cuttings which my dad has kept all these years

scraps

THE OFFICIAL MAGAZINE
LIVERPOOL

School for survival

Club History

ESSENTIAL READING FOR ALL TRUE 'REDS'

■ Exclusive interviews
■ Stunning pictures of your Anfield heroes
■ Detailed match reports
■ Fabulous competitions
■ All the latest Anfield news.

Rush's Challenge

FREE!

Available at all good newsagents for only £2.20

...ISER, THURSDAY, FEBRUARY 8, 1951.

Deeside maestros saunter home

by Alan Davies

Swansea Primary Schools 3,
Deeside Primary Schools 3.

THE young footballing maestros of Deeside done it again! They travelled to South Wales at the weekend and out-played a Swansea side in their second live quarter final of the Welsh Yeoman Shield.

And even though Swansea scored two goals in the last eight minutes, the Deesiders had already done enough to saunter on to the semi-final with a 7-2 aggregate.

They hit the home side with everything they had in the opening stages and were close to scoring three times in the first five minutes.

BRILLIANT

Then, after only 10 minutes they thrilled the many sup-porters who had travelled with them with a brilliant goal. The youngsters swept the ball the length of the field with a seven-man move for Gareth Pritchard (Flint Welsh) to hammer a 20-yard shot into the back of the net.

Chris Hewitt and Steven Williams were close to adding to the score as Deeside kept Swansea penned in their own half of the field. And Gary Griffiths (Bryn Deva) made a magnificent save just before the interval to deny Swansea an equaliser.

Deeside's inevitable second goal came early in the second half when the lurking Michael Boden (Queensferry) was on hand to smash home a fierce drive.

Minutes later Chris Hewitt (Sealand) increased the lead. Gareth Pritchard was brought down in the area but advan-tage was played and Hewitt slipped the loose ball into the net.

Ian Rush had the ball in the Swansea net again but the 'goal' was disallowed and then a powerful header by the same player was scooped off the line. Nicholas Furnival and Keith Lewis both went close with the Deeside con-tingent roaring them on.

The Swansea boys hit back with two goals in the final minutes to give the scoreline a respectability their play had never deserved.

Deeside now meet Ebbw Vale or Western Valley in the semi-final with Ebbw holding a 2-1 lead from the first leg.

On Saturday Deeside travel to play East Flintshire and the team will be: Gary Griffiths (Bryn Deva), Keith Massey (Custom House Lane), Michael Bodden and Mark Pickford (Queensferry), Steven Williams (Bagillt Glan Aber), Stephen Lea (Bagillt Merllyn), Chris Hewitt (Sealand), Ian Rush (Flint St. Mary's), Gareth Pritchard (Flint Welsh), Keith Lewis (Queensferry), Barry Horne (Bagillt). Subs: Aberi, Tim Williams (Flint Welsh), Gareth Mason (Taliesin, and Nicholas Furni-vall (Queensferry).

SCHOOLBOYS MAKE IT 19 ON THE TROT

by Alan Davies

East Flintshire Primary School 1, Deeside Primary Schools 6.

DEESIDE chalked up their 19th win in a row when they completed the double over East Flintshire at Hawarden.

They set off at a cracking pace and rocked the home side with two goals in the first five minutes. The first came when Keith Lewis (Queensferry) was put clear by a fine pass by Ian Rush (Flint St. Mary's) and minutes later Rush netted the second direct from a corner.

Deeside's fast, flowing football had the East Flintshire defence at sixes and sevens and they went further ahead when the alert Rush seized on a loose ball after the home 'keeper had parried a powerful drive by Chris Hewitt.

East Flintshire hit back and were rewarded with a goal from a fierce shot from the right wing which left Deeside keeper Gary Griffiths rooted to his line.

But Deeside were un-daunted by this setback and further goals by Gareth Pritchard (Flint Welsh) and Chris Hewitt (Sealand) gave them a commanding interval lead.

In the second half youngsters from Deeside complete masters but only created many chances. The goal came late in the game from Stephen Lea (Bagillt Merllyn) after fine work by the unselfish Rush.

Deeside travel to ... corn Primary Schools Saturday.

The team will be: Gary Griffiths (Bryn Deva), Keith Massey and Ian Brereton (Custom House Lane), Michael Pickford (Queensferry), Steven Williams (Bagillt Glan Aber), Stephen Lea (Bagillt Merllyn), Ian Chris Hewitt (Sealand), Ian Rush (Flint St. Mary's), Gareth Pritchard (Flint Welsh), Keith Lewis (Queensferry), Barry Horne (Bagillt Welsh).

Eight-goal boost for a cup clash

Deeside Primary Schools 8,
Shrewsbury Primary Schools 1

DEESIDE'S footballing youngsters kept up their march on the path for honours with yet another resounding victory at the expense of Shrewsbury.

And this encouraging display, one of the best of the season, should put the seal on their confident mood for the Welsh Yeoman Shield first leg semi-final tie with Ebbw Vale in South Wales ... Saturday.

... Chris Hewitt (Sealand) put Deeside ... in the 10th minute, and ... Pritchard (Flint Welsh) put them ... from a penalty after Hewitt had ... brought down in the area.

The home side scored a third ... before the interval, when fast Br... was palmed out by the goal... brought to the feet of the lurking ... (Bagillt Merllyn). Lea made ... from close range.

RUSH HAT-TRICK

In the second half the splen... Rush (Flint St. Mary's) helped hi... a hat-trick, his third goal coming ...

move in which Deeside swept the length of the field.

Gareth Pritchard scored the seventh, and Lee ended the scoring with a tremen-dous shot from the wing.

Shrewsbury rallied near the end and ... a consolation goal in the dying ...

Scorer of all eight goals in St. Mary's 8-4 win over Gwynedd School—that's Ian Rush.

Deeside Primary Schools extended their winning run ... 23 games this season when ... beat Chester City Schools at Queensferry on Saturday.

FOOTBALL WIN FOR ST. MARY'S

On Tuesday afternoon of last week St. Mary's team played football against Bryn Deva School team, Connah's Quay School team. The score was St. Mary's 4 goals, Bryn Deva 1 goal. Ian Rush scored the four goals. The team was C. Pickering, P. Roberts, R. Dixon, W. Brown, S. H. Jones, M. Fennah, K. Feeney, P. Rush, I. Rush, P. Stenhoff, A. James. Sub, M. ...

In the quarter-finals of the Tom Roberts' Cup match, St. Mary's played Pen Morfa School, Prestatyn. The result was a draw, four goals each. St. Mary's have now been given a replay for the replay. This is the first point that St. Mary's have forfeited in both cup and league fixtures since the start of the season. The team was C. Pickering, R. Dixon, S. Brown, K. Humphreys, M. Fennah, K. Feeney, James, M. Fennah, P. Rush, I. Rush, M. Nuttall, P. Stenhoff, Sub, V. James, Sub. I. Roberts. The referee was Mr. J. Travers.

11-GOAL SCHOOLBOYS STILL UNBEATEN

DEESIDE PRIMARY
SCHOOLS 11
CHESTER RURAL
PRIMARY SCHOOLS 0

Deeside stretched their un-beaten record this season to 17 games with a win when they completely overwhelmed the Chester side, who admitted that they had lost the match before even kick-off.

Five minutes after the start Keith Lewis shot home after Queensferry made a great run. Keith Lewis then shot from Queensferry, Keith Lewis, in the 8th Rush and Boden have his fee...

Lewis scored a second time afterwards and then Ian Rush (St. Mary's) came into his own with a well-played third for the home side a comfortable 4-0 lead at the interval.

The second half saw Dee-side strengthen their hold and run riot with four more goals. Keith Lewis netting his third ... a fine solo run, then set up chances for Boden, Boden, two, one with a great shot, the other nearly done...

SATURDAY'S GAME

A quiet match is expected at Queensferry on Saturday. Kick-off 10.45 ... Boden ... known to have a great day, and Deeside will only need a ... of their best to register a vic-tory.

Later, Nicholas Furnival (Queensferry) intercepted the ...

Deeside in a rush

3.14 schedule Primary
Schools 9. Deeside
Primary Schools 4. a fast trick by Ian Rush (Flint
St. Mary's), two goals
from Gareth Pritchard
(Flint Welsh) and one
(Bagillt Merllyn) saw
Deeside Primary victory
over East Flintshire...
tory in the first leg of the
Welsh Yeoman Shield
competition.

The second leg will be played at Queensferry on Saturday, December 30 and the winners will play Swansea.

Deeside strikers run riot

DEESIDE PRIMARY
SCHOOLS 9
CRECCE PRIMARY
SCHOOLS 1

For a long time the first half Crecce seemed to hold their own and put up a bold front while their defence heroically cracked under the home ram.

In the opening 20 minutes before Rush and Boden got going with Rush and Boden (Flint Welsh) reduced the two back.

FOUR MORE

Deeside forced its way into the Crecce defence time and time again, only to be foiled by their tactics and Rush ...

PENALTY DECISION

In the last minute a harsh penalty decision went against the defending side and Llandudno scored their second...

Saturday Deeside have ... agreed previously to visit ... Barmouth.

Crecce team: ... M. Gar... (Bryn Deva). Keith Massey (Custom House Lane), Ian Brereton (Queensferry), Ian Brereton (Queensferry), Michael Boden and Mark Pickford (Queensferry), Williams (Bagillt Glan-Aber), Stephen Lea (Bagillt Merllyn), Chris Hewitt (Sealand), Ian Rush (Flint St. Mary's), Gareth Pritchard (Flint Welsh), Stephen Lea (Bagillt), Keith Lewis (Queensferry), Ian Rush (Flint St. Mary's), Gareth Pritchard (Flint Welsh), Stephen Lea (Bagillt), Chris Hewitt (Sealand), Subs: Aberi, Gareth Mason (Taliesin), Nicholas Furnival (Queensferry), Barry Horne (Bagillt Welsh).

Deeside boys must be firm favourites

IN the Yeoman Shield, first round, first leg game played at Llandudno last Saturday morning, Dee-side built up a useful lead which should stake them favourites to win the tie when the second leg is played at Queensferry on Saturday, December 30 (10.30 am).

The winners play home and away against Swansea, at Llandudno. Deeside took an early lead. Ian Rush (Flint St. Mary's) was on hand to twice after a shot from Keith Lewis had been parried by the home keeper. Lewis was prominent again as he made headway against the fast-flowing feature of the game.

From another corner Ian Rush headed cleverly and Rush headed home with more power and deceptive after being set clear by Michael ...

Before half time Deeside and Crecc Welsh' leading ... one another from close ...

In the second half ... back heart of the goal ... bundled over to ... were easily. More ... (Bagillt Merllyn) scored ...

Llandudno Primary Schools 2
Deeside Primary Schools 4

number five with a fine close range following inter-esting play by Deeside and Pritchard both and to have ... set their goals.

Michael Boden (Queens-ferry) also scored when he ... a drive was netted into ...

The Deeside team, chosen for the game at Bryn Grif-fiths (Bryn Deva), Keith Mas-sey and Ian Brereton (Custom House Lane), Michael Boden and Mark Pickford (Queens-ferry), Gareth Pritchard (Flint Welsh), Gareth Pritchard (Flint Welsh), Keith Lewis (Queensferry), Ian Rush (Flint St. Mary's), Steven Williams (Bagillt Glan-Aber) and Chris Hewitt (Sealand). Substitute: Nicholas Furnival (Taliesin), Gareth Mason (Taliesin), Aberi, Barry Horne (Glan Aber).

These boys are great

On Saturday at Queens-ferry (10.30) Deeside Primary Schools play their keen-est game in the All-Wales Yeo-man Shield competition.

They play Llandudno, recent winners over Aberystwyth, in the first leg, the return being at Llandudno a week on Saturday, if successful the tie will be at a twelve Scorers only in the New Year, Rush will with under ... high left and goal only the goals scored ... against only six forwards, all to find a goal record in their efforts to bring result is what they are to be playing for a good ... of North Wales for the first time.

Games are played at ... Crecc ... Bryn Deva, Welsh, Bagillt, Bagillt Glan-Aber, Queensferry, ...

RUSH TO HARDEN

THAT was the week that was for Flint's new star, young Ian Rush, who broke the ... record of ... goals in ... game ...

An identical story ... big week the bigger ... that ... Harden ...

Proud Ian shows off cup medal

Flint fan Rush was ... which the Deeside Primary Schools play... a great season ...

Deeside school ... pos... against Deesi... for the replay ... so by m... out ... ...

Nothing had been ...

Shrewsbury attack at their best had been under constant ... and the home keeper was more than a spectator.

In the second half ... (Flint St. Mary's) was rewarded with his whole hearted display with a great hat trick. His opportunist third goal was a constant threat as he brilliantly with the home ... His last goal was the result in which Deeside swept the length of the field. Gareth ... helped himself to ... with a tremendous ... wing and generally ... no answer to the ... applied by the home ... end the visitors and Mason (Taliesin) in ... was called upon to ... lent user. Soon ... ever, Mason was ...

THAT day the week that was for Flint's new star, young Ian Rush, who broke the ... record of ... goals in ... game ...

Field Of Dreams

This is the field where I used to play football all the time when I was a boy.

I lived around the corner in a council house in Woodfield Avenue. I'd play out and hang around the streets a lot, especially in the summertime, because all I wanted to do was play football or cricket. We'd even play golf on the school field, though we only had one or two golf clubs. It was a way of life. You look back now and it sounds like it wasn't a good thing, but that's what it was like. We had to fight hard for what we got. Nothing came easy for us. My mum and dad worked really hard to give us what they could. The local community was very good. Everyone helped each other.

People around here are very proud people. They're a bit like Liverpool people. You can't put a price on friendliness and helping each other.

Everton FC

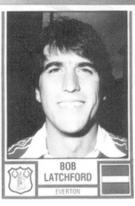

BOB LATCHFORD

EVERTON

	Games	(Goals)
EVERTON.......	236	(106)
ENGLAND.......	12	(5)
CAREER..........	546	(231)

Bob Latchford

My Boyhood Hero

I supported Everton as a kid and my hero then was Bob Latchford. The year I started watching them he scored something like 30 goals and Dave Thomas was on the wing. I loved goalscorers at that age so Bob Latchford became my hero.

Watching him made me want to be a goalscorer. I scored a lot of goals playing for Deeside Primary Schools and at secondary school, I just loved finding the net. I think watching Bob Latchford's movement inside the box helped me as player.

We Can Be Heroes, Just For One Day

In the late '70s, early '80s I liked an alternative rock band from North Wales called The Alarm. I used to listen to Human League as well, then I got into Phil Collins who I still really like today. My hero was David Bowie. When I was 14 I even had a David Bowie haircut with ginger hair that was sticking out! Bowie was my hero and I was lucky enough to meet him once. When I got older, Phil Collins was my number one as far as music goes, but for someone like David Bowie to keep going for four decades is incredible. He was something different and I used to get all of his records on vinyl. I've still got them, somewhere.

"HEROES" DAVID BOWIE

No Jacket Required

Phil Collins

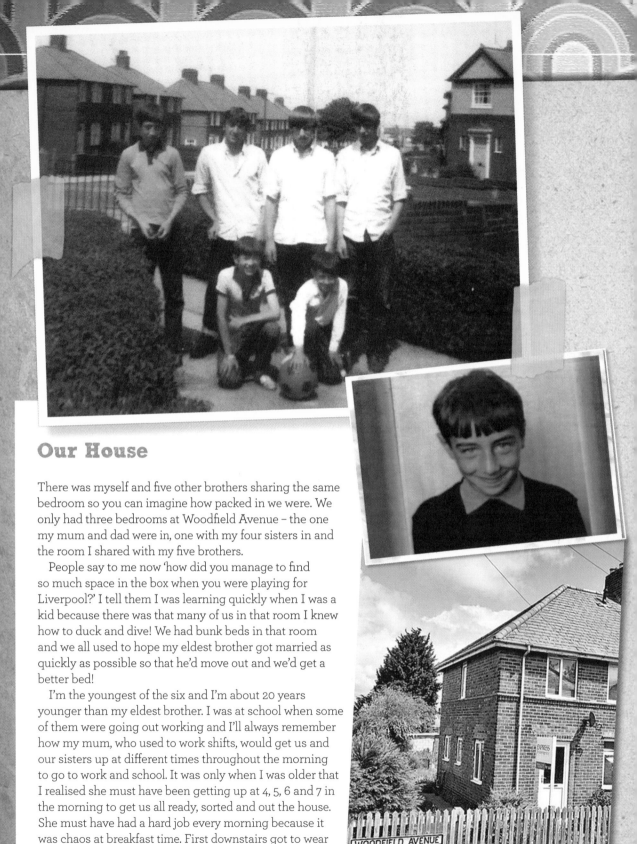

Our House

There was myself and five other brothers sharing the same bedroom so you can imagine how packed in we were. We only had three bedrooms at Woodfield Avenue – the one my mum and dad were in, one with my four sisters in and the room I shared with my five brothers.

People say to me now 'how did you manage to find so much space in the box when you were playing for Liverpool?' I tell them I was learning quickly when I was a kid because there was that many of us in that room I knew how to duck and dive! We had bunk beds in that room and we all used to hope my eldest brother got married as quickly as possible so that he'd move out and we'd get a better bed!

I'm the youngest of the six and I'm about 20 years younger than my eldest brother. I was at school when some of them were going out working and I'll always remember how my mum, who used to work shifts, would get us and our sisters up at different times throughout the morning to go to work and school. It was only when I was older that I realised she must have been getting up at 4, 5, 6 and 7 in the morning to get us all ready, sorted and out the house. She must have had a hard job every morning because it was chaos at breakfast time. First downstairs got to wear the best shoes!

WOODFIELD AVENUE

Soccer School

I never did much homework! I used to do what little work I could and then get out to play football. If I'm being honest, a lot of the time I just didn't do my homework and would end up having to write lines in school – 'I must do my homework,' – over and over again, or I'd end up getting sent to the headmaster.

I must do my homework
I must do my homework
I must do my homework
I must do my homework
I must do m

I Swapped Stickers For The Real Thing

I preferred football over other hobbies like collecting stickers. Having said that, I remember collecting the ESSO coins that featured the England team during the 1970 World Cup.

It Was Bruce Lee Before Gordon Lee

I was always out playing football until it went dark so I didn't see a lot of TV but I used to like Bruce Lee films, martial arts stuff. Action films I enjoyed as well, but for TV it was always sports for me, except for maybe some comedies. When I was 10 though, I remember my dad taking me to Chester Races. From then on I was into horse racing.

Sweet Tooth

I had a lot of chocolate when I was young. People say it's for energy, but I just used to eat it because it was chocolate! I've always loved wine gums as well, they've been a favourite of mine for years, and when I was very young we used to have those gob-stoppers that took about three hours to finish off.

Rushing About On My Raleigh Chopper

The Raleigh Chopper was the coolest bike in town for kids in the 1970s and I was lucky enough to have one. People look back on them now as a cult classic. The handlebars were based on the motorbikes which I remember seeing in the film Easy Rider.

I had two bikes – a Chopper and a Racer. The Racer sticks out in my mind. My brother had a big red Racer and mine was a smaller white one. We were always out on our bikes. We'd go down to the school fields on them to play football. The only thing was someone robbed the Racer! If that was you, can I have it back?

23

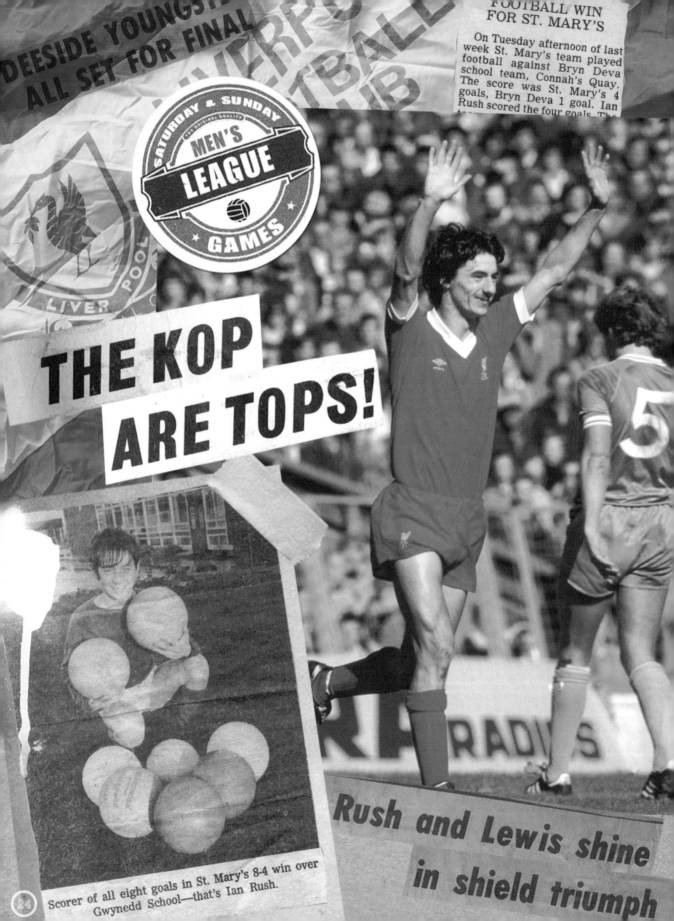

FOOTBALL WIN
FOR ST. MARY'S

On Tuesday afternoon of last week St. Mary's team played football against Bryn Deva school team, Connah's Quay. The score was St. Mary's 4 goals, Bryn Deva 1 goal. Ian Rush scored the four goals. The

SATURDAY & SUNDAY
MEN'S
LEAGUE
GAMES

THE KOP ARE TOPS!

Scorer of all eight goals in St. Mary's 8-4 win over Gwynedd School—that's Ian Rush.

Rush and Lewis shine in shield triumph

The Liverpool terror

ST MARY'S RC PRIMARY

DEESIDE SCHOOLS

CHESTER

LIVERPOOL

DEESIDE Primary Schools pulled off another magnificent win in South Wales on Saturday when they beat Ebbw Vale 4-0 in a semi-final first leg of the Welsh Yeoman Shield.

They are now hot favourites to take the second leg at Queensferry tomorrow (kick-off 10.30) without much trouble and play either Newport or Barry in the final.

Ian Rush (Flint St. Mary's) and Keith Lewis (Queensferry) were Deeside's outstanding forwards. They combined brilliantly in the third minute for Lewis to fire home a great shot past the advancing Vale 'keeper.

Deeside pounded the home goal and Rush raced on to a through ball from Mark Pickford to make it 2-0. Then shots from Stephen Williams, Rush and Lewis crashed against the woodwork.

Just before the interval goalkeeper Gary Griffiths (Bryn Deva) made a great save to deny the Vale a score and Deeside had two more narrow escapes when they scrambled the ball away from their line.

In the second half Deeside attacked for long periods and the home 'keeper covered himself with glory — and mud — with a series of super saves.

My First GAMES

DEESIDE PRIMARY SCHOOLS · 1972?

My First Derby Goal

I was actually playing for the Under-11s when I was seven at St Mary's RC Primary School. I played in a tournament and no-one could believe that I was playing. It was only a one-off, though.

I was very good at everything sporting wise at school. I used to win the running events on sports day and what really helped me was that I was playing football and cricket with my older brothers from such a young age. It became natural for me to play against older lads and that helped me a great deal in my career. It meant I was used to playing against over-age players, so even when I was progressing to play for Wales at schoolboy level, I thought nothing of being in the same team as older lads such as Kevin Ratcliffe.

At St Mary's we only played three or four of our local rivals, but at St. Richard Gwyn Catholic High School we played more often. Our big rivals were Gwynedd and I remember playing two big games against them. In one we won 8-4 and I scored all eight and when we played them away we won 6-1 and I scored the six! It must have put me in good stead to score in Merseyside derbies!

Scorer of all eight goals in St. Mary's 8-4 win over Gwynedd School—that's Ian Rush.

FOOTBALL WIN FOR ST. MARY'S

On Tuesday afternoon of last week St. Mary's team played football against Bryn Deva school team, Connah's Quay. The score was St. Mary's 4 goals, Bryn Deva 1 goal. Ian Rush scored the four goals. The team was C. Pickering, P. Roberts, R. Dixon, W. Brown, S. M. Jones, M. Fennah, A. Fenney, P. Rush, I. Rush, P. Stenhoff, A. James. Sub. M. Nuttall.

In the quarter finals of the Tom Roberts Cup match, St. Mary's played Pen Morfa School, Prestatyn. The result was a draw, four goals each. St. Mary's now have to travel to Prestatyn for the replay. This is the first point that St. Mary's have forfeited in both cup and league fixtures since the start of the season. The team was C. Pickering, R. Dixon, J. Humphreys, W. Brown, S. M. Jones, M. Fennah, A. Fenney, P. Rush, I. Rush, M. Nuttall, A. James. Sub. P. Roberts. The referee was Mr. J. Travers.

We netted 158 goals

The Untouchables

When I was 11, Deeside Primary Schools won everything. We played 33 games and won 33 games, winning the league and the Welsh Cup. John Toshack presented us with our medals. We actually played 32 games, winning all 32, but the only other team from that age-group who had also won all their games that year was Liverpool Schoolboys so we had a one-off game against them to decide which was the best team. We won 5-2 and I scored a hat-trick. I scored 72 goals in total that season, which was a record at the time, beating the 68 scored by a lad called Paul Lewis who went to Queensferry County Primary.

Going into the 32nd game of the season, I'd also scored 68 and our manager, who used to be at Queensferry County Primary, put me as sub! I got 10 minutes, but went on and scored, taking me to 69, and then I got that hat-trick against Liverpool Schoolboys.

Happy winners despite the Arctic conditions – Deeside Primary School team pictured after their Welsh Yeoman Shield match against Swansea at Queensferry recently.

Michael Owen beat my goalscoring record

Michael Owen later beat that record. But I still have some banter with Michael because I only played in 31 games that year whereas he scored about 79 in 42 games. The kid with the most appearances for Deeside Primary Schools was Gary Speed. With the career he had, Gary kept himself remarkably fit.

That's My Boy Scout!

I was mostly up front, especially for Deeside Schools. I scored a lot of goals for them. When I was 13, I think, playing for Flintshire and Wales, they put me on the left side of midfield because they thought I could play there. The rest of the team were a year older so maybe the striker they had was pretty good and they just wanted to fit me in. Funnily enough, I was playing on the left of midfield when a Liverpool scout came to watch me for the first time. He was asking my dad – and he didn't know he was my dad – who I was, but after a few games there I ended up playing up front again and stayed there.

Old Head On Young Shoulders

This would never happen today, but when I was 14 I was playing Sunday League football as well in the same team as two of my brothers. We played for the local Catholic club and I used to play on both the Saturday and the Sunday at one stage. They also used to put me on the left wing, because I was quick, and I'd get kicked to hell – but my brothers and team-mates would help me out.

I think half of the players were still drunk on the Sunday! That must have made it easier for me because I was very quick. We never really won anything, I think maybe one cup – it was more a matter of me getting out there and playing against older people.

That toughened me up and prepared me for going to Chester. I think kids these days are too scared of getting injured, but it didn't do me any harm. I'm not saying kids should go and play overage football at 14 now either, things are completely different, but it was a good education for me. I just used to love playing and would look forward to 11 o'clock every Saturday and Sunday morning from the ages of 14 to 16 because that's when the games were.

Rush for titles

THE football family Rush have really made their mark on the Merseyside and North Wales soccer scene this year.

Ian, (20), led the assault with a stunning show of marksmanship. Liverpool's star centre forward had notched up 30 goals before Saturday's title winning game with Spurs.

Following in his footsteps is fellow striker Stephen (22), who helped steer Rhyl to the runners-up spot in division two of the Cheshire League.

Midfielder Grahame, (23), is part of the Greenfield team set to clinch top in the first division of the Welsh League.

Peter (25), has been a regular midfield player with Flint Town who look set to finish fourth in the first division of the Welsh League.

The lads from Flint were licked into shape at an early age by dad Francis.

The Rush brigade: Ian (centre); Graham (left), Stephen (right), and Peter (back).

My big brothers looked after me when I played in the same Sunday League team as them when I was only 14. When I was at Liverpool they were all still playing football to a decent standard

Cleaning Up At Cheste[r]

I'd been training with the Chester first team from the age of 14. Cliff Sear, the youth team manager, was a big influence on my career. He only took five or six of us on so because there wasn't that many of us, we got to train with the Reserves and the first team. So, when I was 16 and went to Chester as an apprentice, it wasn't that big a thing. I knew what to expect. I was even put in the first team in pre-season for a friendly against Bangor City.

The hardest thing was that I had to get in at nine o'clock, train and then after training clean the changing rooms, players' boots and all that. I was getting home at five or six o'clock at night and all I would do is get something to eat and fall asleep because it was taking that much out of me. For the first three months it was difficult to adjust, but it became a normal thing when I got used to training every day.

Ian in a rush

FLINT schoolboy, Ian Rush, had a busy day on Tuesday.

Ian, a 15-year-old pupil at the Sir Richard Gwyn School, played for the school's soccer team in morning and afternoon games and then had a date with Chester in an F.A. Youth Cup match against Macclesfield at Sealand Road.

He ended an eventful 24 hours by scoring two of the goals and making another in Chester's 4-0 victory.

Over the weekend Ian, who signed schoolboy forms for Chester earlier this season, played for the Wales under 15 team before a 30,000 crowd against ... Paris. The

...ester FC Youth Team Manager Cliff Sear supervises apprentices David Gregory, Paul ...dham (standing), Ian Edwards and Ian Rush (kneeling), as they prepare the Sealand Road pitch for Wednesday's League Cup game with Port Vale.

8 MAR 1980

Rush heads for a record

Ian Rush

Even when he's not scoring goals, good reports continue to come through about the progress and potential of Chester's exciting young discovery, Ian Rush.

The 18-year-old Flint boy, named this week in the Welsh youth squad for the U.E.F.A. tournament, is probably the best player Chester have produced since centre forward Ron Davies, who came from the village of Brynford, near Holywell, and went on to a distinguished career as a First Division star and Welsh international.

But Rush's path looks certain to take a different route than his famous predecessor—if negotiations currently in progress work out as expected. If they do, he'll join Liverpool.

The stumbling block at the moment is routine in these transfer matters. Liverpool rate the lad at a lower price than Chester, who are holding out for more.

Eventually, I believe Rush will come to Anfield at a fee in the region of £250,000—a record for an 18-year old. But, if Chester demand more, there are other clubs interested who may be prepared to agree with Chester's view.

It was all very different when Davies was sold 18 years ago. Both Liverpool and Everton failed to cash in on the Davies potential, although both Bill Shankly and Harry Catterick, the respective managers at that time, had the Welsh lad watched regularly.

Instead of grabbing this up and coming star, he was allowed to slip through the net. Chester sold him to Second Division Luton Town in 1962 for a miserable looking £10,000—one of the biggest giveaways of the post-war years.

Now Chester rate Rush as a £300,000 player and believe there is a First Division club ready to pay that. But I think the lure of Anfield will prove a key factor and the deal taking him to Liverpool should break by next May.

Liverpool have also shown some interest in another teenage striker from the lower divisions—Walsall's Don Penn. They won't sign both of them and they won't take part in an auction for either. Both these youngsters are in the same price range and Liverpool are due to make their annual move into the transfer market for new talent.

Liverpool and Chester have had talks, but not conclusive ones, about Rush. They began at chairman level between good friends John Smith and Reg Rowlands, continued at managerial level between Bob Paisley and Alan Oakes. Each club knows where each other stand.

They have gone a certain part of the way in negotiating a deal but it's not settled yet. while Chester have promotion hopes, a final decision is delayed. But there'll be a new player with a four-letter name on Liverpool's books at the end of the season.

Incidentally, Davies' original fee of £10,000 was made to look paltry as his value soared. Chester are not making the same mistake again of under-valuing a player.

Luton sold Davies to Norwich in less than a year for £35,000, and then Southampton bought him for a then club record fee of £50,000. He was rated at the £200,000 level during his seven years with Saints before signing for Portsmouth when he was 30 for nearly £40,000—four times the amount Chester received when he was 21.

I used to clean Bob Delgado's boots. I still see him now and he's made up that I used to clean his boots. If they weren't cleaned properly there were two ways he'd tell me. He'd either throw me in the bath, fully clothed, or get the boot polish and put them on certain parts that I'm not going to get into! That was what they used to do, then – it was a way of bringing you up. When we turned professional we'd do the same kind of things to the lads cleaning our boots, it was how it was.

Times have changed. Even kids of 13 and 14 who I see at The Academy now have kit-men getting their kit out. It's just the way the world is now and while you wouldn't want them getting thrown in baths and all that, at times they can miss out on what real life is all about. A lot of these kids are not going to make it as professional footballers and have to go into the real world after that. We were lucky in that we'd learnt what the real world was like when we were apprentices. That was a big help for us.

Bob presenting a trophy. Soon I was to be cleaning his boots

First Team Education

My debut was against Sheffield Wednesday at the end of the 1978/79 season. It was quite big for me because Sheffield Wednesday had just been promoted so they brought a lot of fans to Sealand Road. Alan Oakes, the player-manager, played me on the left of midfield instead of playing himself. We drew 2-2 and I hardly got a kick of the ball. He just wanted to give me an education of what it's like to play in the first team.

The following season I couldn't see myself getting in the Chester first team because there was a lad called Ian Edwards there who was playing for Wales and scored five goals in one game at Wrexham. I was thinking 'I'll never get ahead of him' and there was also Ian Howat and Ian Mellor, Neil Mellor's dad, who'd just come in from Man City. Alan Oakes then sold Ian Edwards to Wrexham for £125,000 because he knew he had me to come in. That gave me the confidence to go on to do better things.

Hitting The Goal Trail

My first goal for Chester was memorable, although it was like most of my goals – a tap-in! We were losing 2-1 in the 1979/80 season at Gillingham and I came on as sub to score the equaliser. Sometimes when you come on as a sub you feel more tired coming off the pitch and can't get your second breath.

I remember coming off the pitch at Gillingham and the kit-man, Vince Pritchard – who was as hard as nails – was making me tidy all the kit up ready for him because I was still an apprentice. I was absolutely knackered, but he said *'even though you've scored a goal you've still got to do your job'.* So while all the players were getting a shower, I was cleaning their kit up.

Reds Capture £300-a-week Rushie

ranges Jaff

I'VE ARRIVED . . . but it's only the start for Ian Rush at Anfield.

Paisley first in the rush

By Tim Taylor

LIVERPOOL will have first place in the queue when the inevitable auction gets under way for £750,000-rated Chester superboy Ian Rush.

With typical Anfield forethought, Bob Paisley has claimed first option on the 18-year-old former Welsh schoolboy international who has scored 11 goals in 14 games within three months of signing his first professional contract.

It was only on Saturday that Rush played at his first major soccer stadium when he scored in Third Division Chester's 2—0 F.A. Cup upset at Newcastle.

Rush was watched by Liverpool at Newcastle.

Meanwhile a player tipped as a future Anfield star— Howard Gayle, the 20-year-old coloured Liverpool winger, starts a month's loan with Fulham at the end of the week.

YEOVIL goalkeeper Brian P the day his side lo Cup. The 25-year-old former A on Saturday night too late to on BBC's Match of the Day.

Parker's day became a co dentally caught flush in the Robson's right boot. He spent cussion and double vision.

Printed and Published by Expr Registered as a Newspaper at th

RUSH HITS THE ROAD TO FAME

TEENAGE striker Ian Rush donned a Liverpool shirt yesterday and set out on the path he hopes will lead to soccer stardom with Liverpool.

While the champions were concentrating on their FA Cup semi-final second replay with Arsenal, Rush travelled over from Chester to Anfield for a medical, and after passing it quickly signed the forms that completed a £330,000 deal—making him the most expensive 18-year-old in British football.

He said: 'My ambition now is to get a place in Liverpool's first team.'

And he has plenty of examples to follow, like Kevin Keegan and Ray Clemence, who were both snapped up from lower divisions before finding fame and fortune at Liverpool.

COLIN WOOD

RUSH SET TO SIGN

LIVERPOOL expect to complete the signing today of Chester's promising teenage striker Ian Rush. The champions have already agreed terms of £300,000 and, if Rush signs after a medical and talks at Anfield this morning he will become the most expensive 18-year-old in British football.

He played his last game for Chester in the victory over Southend on Saturday and said afterwards: 'I am sorry to leave such a great bunch of lads who have done a lot for me. But my ambition now is to get into the first team at Liverpool.'

NO RUSH, IAN!

By PETER FITTON

IAN RUSH knows he may not be able to live up to his surname by making an instant impact at Liverpool.

But that didn't stop the 18-year-old Chester striker signing for the Anfield club yesterday in a £300,000 deal, rubber stamping negotiations manager Bob Paisley completed midway through the season.

For all his growing reputation as one of the goal kings of the future, the Welsh Under-21 international must obey the slow process to First Division recognition that even Kevin Keegan had to follow at Liverpool.

The Mersey giants won the transfer race for Rush, scorer of 17 goals so far this season, from many top clubs including Manchester City and Spurs.

THE DAY I SIGNED FOR LFC

It was crazy, really. When I was scoring goals regularly for Chester, I started seeing stories in the papers saying people were looking at me, but I didn't believe it. I just got on with my game. So when Liverpool came in, Alan Oakes pulled me to one side at an away game and said 'what would you do if someone came in for you?' I said 'I don't want to go'. So he said 'what would it take for you to stay? £100-a-week?'

I was on £40-a-week at the time so I was well happy, and when Liverpool came in for me, I turned them down because I didn't think I was good enough. I wasn't ready. There was talk of Man City, when Malcolm Allison was there, but he said I wasn't ready. Everton also came in and the manager, Gordon Lee, said I wasn't good enough. But Liverpool were still interested.

Alan Oakes went with me and my dad to Anfield, where we met Bob Paisley. Bob offered £300-a-week plus a signing on fee. I was happy with £100-a-week! Bob then took us down to Melwood in his car to watch the first team train and brought us back to Anfield for a meal with the players. I always remember Alan Oakes saying 'you might as well go, give it a chance. If you don't like it you can always come back to Chester'. He also said 'I'll guarantee you one thing. In your first year you'll hate it, but if you come through that first year, it's the best lifestyle you'll ever have.'

He was 100% right because in the first year, I did hate it, but once the penny dropped, I was lucky enough to get a chance and take it. I never looked back after that and I'll always say it's the best career you can ever have if you love playing football. People play for nothing, so to get well paid to do it was a dream come true, but without the help of my dad and Alan Oakes it might never have happened.

Plenty In Reserve

My first goal for Liverpool Reserves was at Blackpool in May 1980 because it was just after I'd signed for them. I think Ronnie Whelan, Howard Gayle and Kevin Sheedy were in the team that day. Liverpool had won the Reserve League and it was a boiling hot day – I think it was Bank Holiday Monday – although I don't remember the goal. I do remember realising that day that I was now playing with good players, even in the Reserves. We had players like Colin Irwin and Steve Ogrizovic in that team, great players.

Alan Oakes, my manager at Chester, had a big influence on my career

Liverpool goals as they clinched their 100th Central League title with a 3—3 draw at Blackpool.

King For A Day

My full debut for Liverpool was at Ipswich in December 1980. Funnily enough I wore the number seven shirt that day. Kenny was injured. We went down there and I played up front with David Johnson, but after 20 minutes he got injured as well so I ended up playing up front alongside Sammy Lee! We drew 1-1.

Sammy was really good to me when I first arrived. I was very shy and Sammy, being a typical Scouser, tried to help me. I never used to say anything back then so I think that's probably why Bob Paisley put Sammy alongside me because I was closest to him and he helped me to get through the game. Kenny got fit again after that and I wasn't seen in the first team again for another three months.

My first
YOU'LL NEVER WALK ALONE
LIVERPOOL
game

My LFC debut Ipswich v Liverpool, December 1980

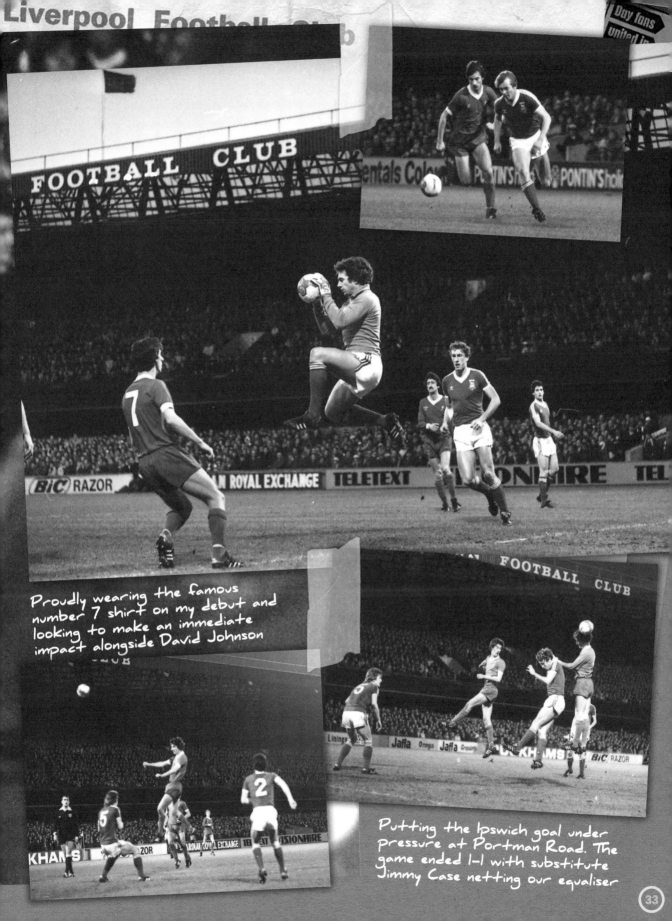

Proudly wearing the famous number 7 shirt on my debut and looking to make an immediate impact alongside David Johnson

Putting the Ipswich goal under pressure at Portman Road. The game ended 1-1 with substitute Jimmy Case netting our equaliser

33

nas period have placed
them safely alongside the
promotion prospectors

TEENAGE striker Ian
donned a Liverp...
and...

brothers are also
players ...
ed the game as a
...lboy with the
Deeside Primary
Schools team that
went through ...

...ich is geared to
blood young players in
the reserves before
putting them in the
first team.
Ian, who is C...

My LFC debut: Ipswich v Liverpool, December 1980

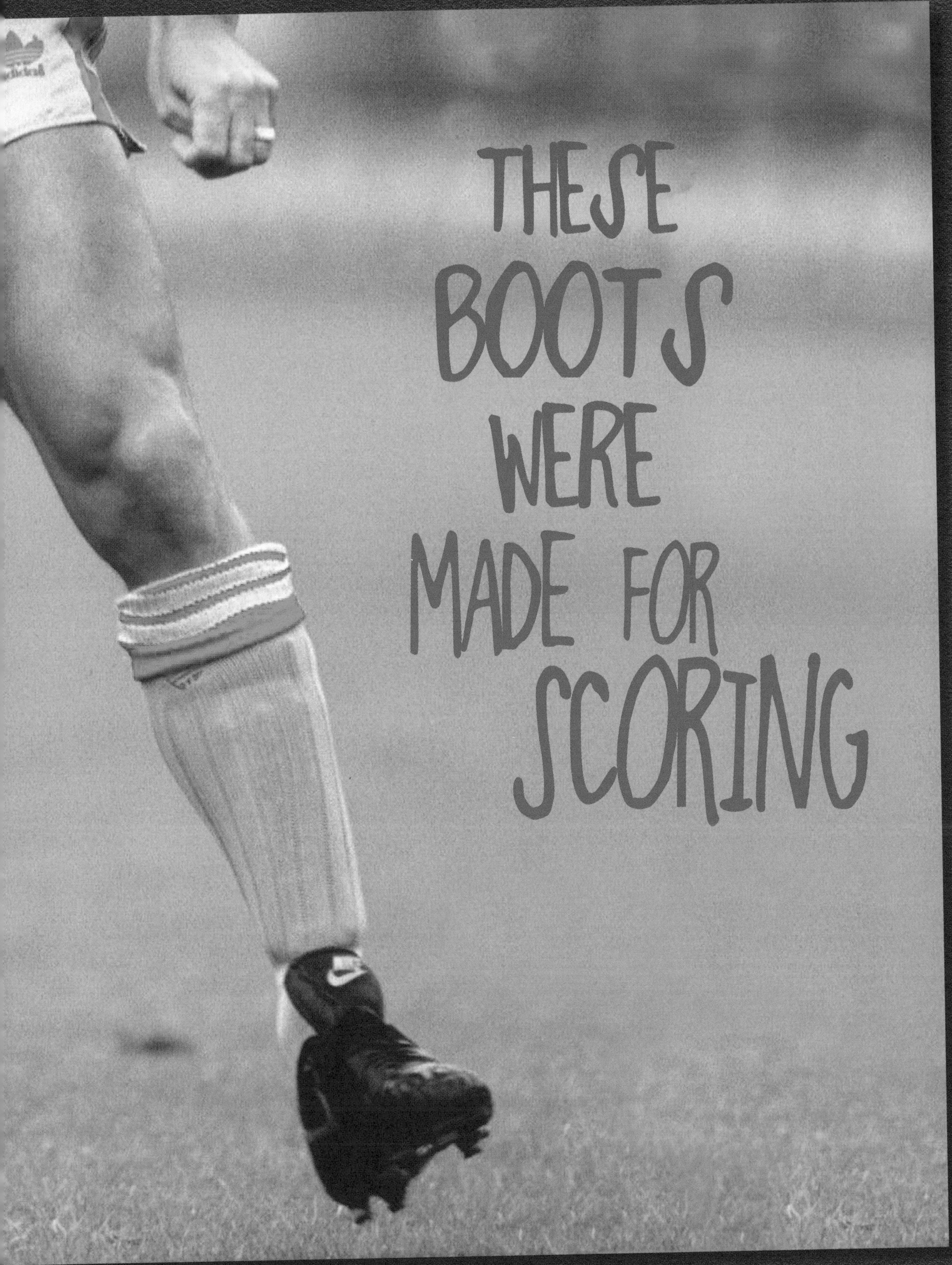

THESE
BOOTS
WERE
MADE FOR
SCORING

Having A Ball In My White Boots

My first pair of boots were white, just like Alan Ball's at Everton.

It was really unusual in those days because everybody else had black boots, but I thought they were really special.

In this day and age, players seem to have all sorts of multi-coloured boots and you are more likely to be the odd one out if you have black ones.

My TOP BOOTS

Nike Tiempo

When I started playing at Chester City I wore adidas, but when I went to Liverpool my mate Jim Pearson, who used to work for Nike, asked me to try some of their boots out.

I was the first player to wear Nike boots in the UK and I've had a bond with Nike ever since.

They've given me a contract for life because I stayed with them in the early '80s when I could've gone to different companies.

This boot is the Nike Tiempo. With the Tiempo I really noticed the difference when wearing them in the early '80s because they were based on my feet!

Nike came and took impressions and measurements of my feet and basically based the Tiempo on that. The leather was a bit different too and I found them very comfortable to play in.

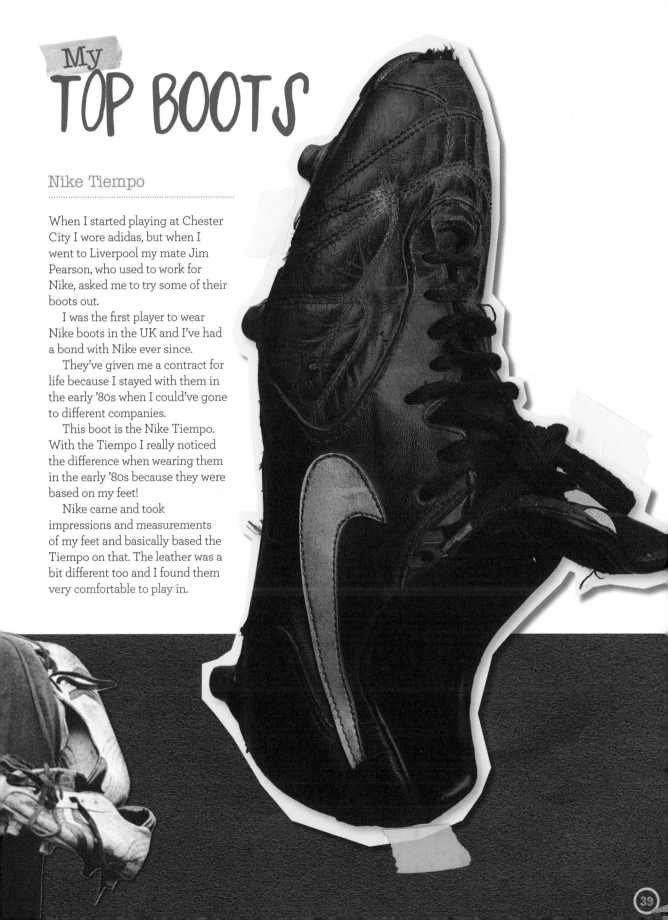

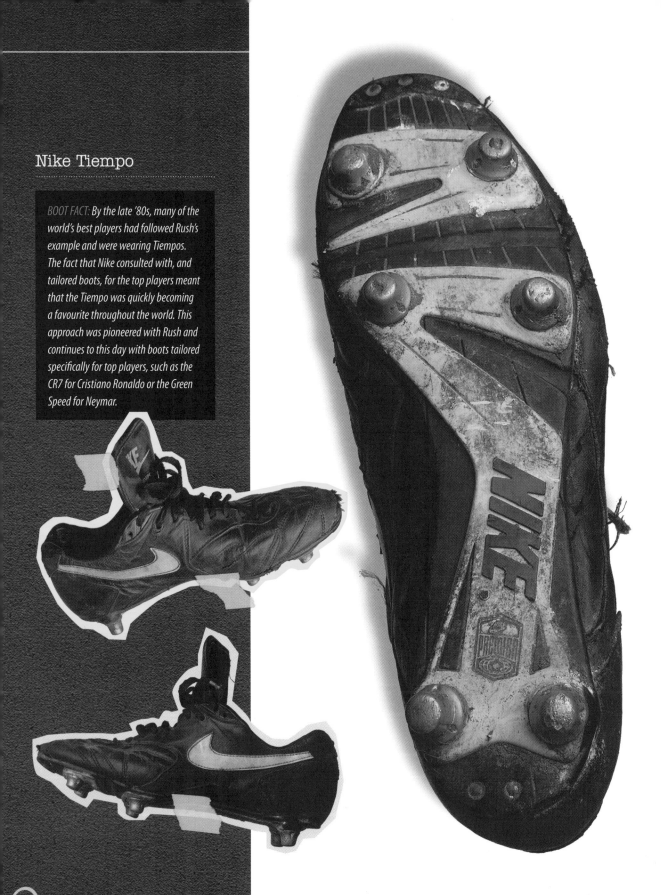

Nike Tiempo

BOOT FACT: By the late '80s, many of the world's best players had followed Rush's example and were wearing Tiempos. The fact that Nike consulted with, and tailored boots, for the top players meant that the Tiempo was quickly becoming a favourite throughout the world. This approach was pioneered with Rush and continues to this day with boots tailored specifically for top players, such as the CR7 for Cristiano Ronaldo or the Green Speed for Neymar.

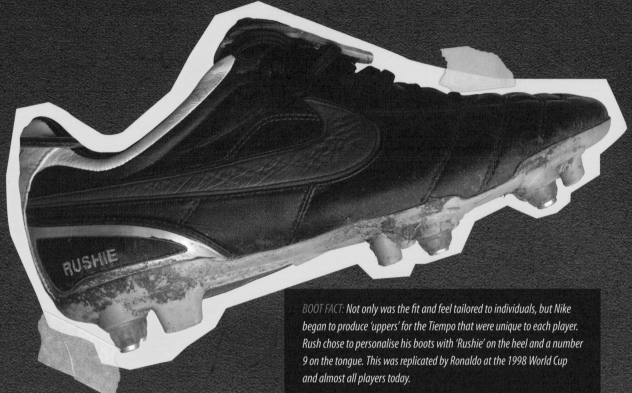

BOOT FACT: Not only was the fit and feel tailored to individuals, but Nike began to produce 'uppers' for the Tiempo that were unique to each player. Rush chose to personalise his boots with 'Rushie' on the heel and a number 9 on the tongue. This was replicated by Ronaldo at the 1998 World Cup and almost all players today.

Nike Tiempo Premier

In the 1990s Nike developed a new boot, the Tiempo Premier, and again they based it on my feet. I have wider feet than a lot of people and that made these boots great for me.

It was at the time when boot companies first started putting players' names on the boots and Nike put 'Rushie' near to the heel of these boots and the number 9 on the tongue as well. It was great to see that.

Again, the studs were different on these boots. This particular pair have got both studs and moulded studs, which was a new design at the time.

Some people like playing in just moulded boots, but I preferred studs to be honest, especially on matchdays.

I often trained in moulded boots but then wore studs on a matchday, maybe because I'm superstitious!

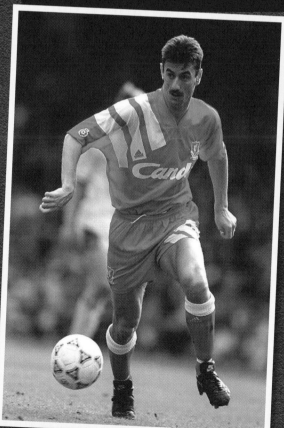

Nike Limited Edition

These are my most up-to-date boots and the leather has changed so much on these compared to the early days of Nike.

This is the a Nike Tiempo Limited Edition boot and as you can see they've got 'Rush 9' printed on the tongue. The '94' printed next to them marks the year when Nike decided to take soccer, as they call it, seriously because the World Cup was in the USA.

As I said, this boot is a limited edition model bearing my name and the only other two players who they made these boots for were Romario and Paolo Maldini.

*In off the Red:
An advert
I did for Nike*

BOOT FACT: *For the 1994 World Cup in the USA, Nike decided to release a limited gold edition of the Nike Tiempo boots based on three football legends. I was lucky enough to be chosen as one of them and the other two were Romario and Maldini. I still wear these boots now when I'm playing in Masters games and charity matches.*

Taking part in a charity game

Paolo Maldini and Romario during the '94 World Cup

I didn't play in that World Cup but it was a reward for me for sticking with Nike throughout my career and at their headquarters in Oregon they actually have a car parking space for me.

Saying that, the great Michael Jordan had a building named after him there and that sounds more impressive!

Nike have been really loyal to me and provided me with some great boots. I play in moulded ones now because I'm getting older and don't play in many games, but I still wear Tiempo to hopefully keep the goalscoring going.

HE GETS THE BALL HE SCORES A GOAL.. IAN, IAN RUSH

All of the goals I scored were important but some stick in the memory more than others. Here are a few from my first spell at Anfield

There were mixed emotions on the night I scored my first goal for Liverpool

Thanks Shanks
30.09.81

v Oulu Palloseura, Anfield, European Cup

My first goal for Liverpool was scored on an emotional night at Anfield. This was the first game after news broke of Bill Shankly's sudden and unexpected death.

At least we did the great man proud by recording a 7-0 win against Oulu Palloseura in the European Cup.

I was left unmarked six yards out and poked in a simple effort to get my Liverpool tally up and running. It wouldn't be the last time I would score from such close range.

A few days later, John Toshack's Swansea would visit Anfield and the Kop paid a raucous tribute to their messiah. I didn't find the net but I was on the scoresheet twice in the next game – a 5-0 defeat of Exeter City in the League Cup.

Wembley First

13.03.82

**v Tottenham Hotspur,
Wembley, League Cup Final**

How could I not include my first goal
at Wembley? I ran through on goal,
fed David Johnson and although
Ray Clemence smothered his effort, I
managed to get the ball back and swept
home from 10 yards.

06.11.82
v Everton, Goodison Park, Football League Division One

Rush Scored One...

This was the derby that made history and it doesn't need explaining to most Liverpool fans of a certain age! It all started when Alan Hansen charged forward and produced a perfect pass which allowed me to get behind Everton's defence and my first-time shot was good enough to beat Neville Southall.

Rush Scored Two...

For my second goal, Hansen was involved again as he passed to me about 20 yards from goal and my shot took a slight deflection and bobbled into the Everton goal – not that I was complaining!

Rush Scored Three...

Kenny laid on an inch-perfect ball to set up a one-on-one for number three. Although my initial shot hit the post, I managed to fire home the rebound to seal my hat-trick – the first in a Merseyside derby since 1935.

And Rush Scored Four

It was Sammy Lee with the pinpoint ball this time as he set me off on another one-on-one. I raced through on goal, rounded Southall and calmly finished to seal a brilliant performance from the lads.

'I rounded Southall and calmly finished to seal a brilliant performance from the lads'

Mark Lawrenson rises after scoring Liverpool's third to accept the congratulations of Craig Johnston and Ian Rush.

Collection time for keepers

Bruce Grobbelaar takes some stick hitting back some of the coins thrown at him — while Neville Southall wasn't driven to drink, but had to retrieve a bottle.

Too cruel

THERE was a time in football's fashionable sixties when results like this one merely salted the theatre of Merseyside's tense sporting rivalry.

The same can no longer be said. The 17th derby did the city no favours. Everton's humiliation was total and disturbing to the extent that one sensed a creeping embarrassment in Liverpool's departure from Goodison.

Everton did not so much surrender as threw down their weapons and took on a Sherman tank with a pocket-knife. They performed like pale immitators of themselves, without confidence or purpose, as if intimidated by Liverpool's unfussed disregard for the traditional tension.

The inevitable massacre left a question mark over Everton's ability to perform on the big occasion, territory they must tread if the club is to regain the prestige of an era past and give the city the second

<table>
<tr><td>Everton</td><td>0</td></tr>
<tr><td>Liverpool</td><td>5</td></tr>
</table>

by Nick Hilton
Pictures: Frank Loughlin and Tony Kenwright

dimension of success it needs to face the future.

The day's popular epitaph that "It was men against boys" disguised the reality that Everton's youngsters must sometime find the appetite to take on men's battles; that pride can be as important as ability.

Too many players of reputation were anonymous, a playing pattern was barely discernible. Had this team played so much good football this season? There was some mitigation for Everton's plight,

Bruce Grobbelaar salutes an Ian Rush success.

I should have had six, says Rush

by Ian Ross

IAN RUSH'S four goal blast at Goodison Park ensured him of much more than a match ball souvenir and a broad smile.

The quiet Welshman guaranteed himself a place in Merseyside's hall of footballing fame by becoming only the third player ever to score four goals in a derby match.

Fittingly it has happened once to each club since the first Everton-Liverpool confrontation back in 1894.

Sandy Young, scorer of Everton's winning goal in the 1906 Cup Final, notched four goals against the Reds at Goodison Park two years earlier and Freddie Howe did the same at Anfield in the 1935-36 season when Everton were beaten 6-0.

Despite his obvious delight Rush's match-winning feat was tempered by a disappointment at not scoring even more.

"I could have had six. I hit the bar and missed a couple of chances I should have taken. I still can't really believe it because I haven't scored four goals in one game since my schooldays," he said.

"I hadn't scored in the last seven matches but I never lost my confidence. It's an incredible experience," added Rush

Facts of the match

Shots on goal: Everton 9 (one on target), Liverpool 23 (15 on target)
Corners: Everton 5, Liverpool 4.
Fouls: Everton 10, Liverpool 8.
Offside: Everton 2, Liverpool 16.

who finally managed to claim the match ball after a two hour search.

The 127th Merseyside derby will also be long remembered by 28-year-old Glen Keeley for completely different reasons.

The transfer-listed Blackburn Rovers centreback making his debut for the Blues only a week after starting a month's loan period was sent off by referee Derek Civil after 33 minutes.

Keeley, playing his first senior game since May, fell foul of the new Football League clampdown on professional fouls and was dismissed for holding back Liverpool's Kenny Dalglish just outside the penalty area.

"I took a gamble. It was simply instinct. I just grabbed him. I was a little bit disappointed to be sent off but I have no complaints. I can't grumble," he said.

Everton boss Howard Kendall, who surprised many by bringing Keeley into the side in place of Mark Higgins, stood by his decision.

"Glen started off well and although I feel sorry for the lad the referee was totally justified in his action.

"It was difficult to assess our performance when we were down to ten men. We had a back four and a goalkeeper but their performance was poor. Teams are getting at us too often. They are going through the middle too quickly. If you have to face someone with only ten men the last opposition you would choose would be Liverpool," he said.

"I felt that even with ten men with the advantage of the wind in the second half

that we could put them under pressure and get the goal back. Unfortunately they got the goal we needed," he added.

Liverpool manager Bob Paisley's only comment was: "Yes, we deserved to win. Yes, I am happy."

Reds' captain Graeme Souness said the last thing his team-mates would do after such an emphatic victory was gloat.

"You will not find us gloating about this and I am not being patronising when I say it could happen to us before the end of the season. We got the breaks today and with Ian Rush in that sort of form anything can happen," he said.

Kevin Sheedy, the former Anfield man who joined Everton before the start of the season, was naturally disappointed.

"The sending off of Glen was a blow but Liverpool deserved their win," he said.

Liverpool goalkeeper Bruce Grobbelaar was the toast of the Everton ballboys after the match when he handed over nearly £7 in coins he had picked up from the Gwladys Street goalmouth.

"The area around the goal was littered in fifty and ten pence pieces. It's no wonder people can't afford to got to two matches a week when they throw their money away," he joked.

Ian Rush slots home the first goal.

Graeme Sharp in a rare Everton attack but B
Grobbelaar collects.

for comfort

though none that would have altered their fate.

The dismissal of central defender Glen Keeley in circumstances which might have been text book written for the new interpretations of the law over the so-called professional foul, reduced them to ten men for two thirds of the game.

The contest however was already lost to Everton when the loaned Blackburn player departed having finally let go of Dalglish's shirt and accepted the inevitable punishment from referee Derek Civil. Ian Rush's eleventh minute opener barely reflected Liverpool's command, the four goals which followed were overdue.

Everton's gamble on their early good fortune, keeping men forward in the hope of an equaliser, collapsed from the moment Rush rifled his second past a curiously flat-footed Neville Southall from 20 yards in the 51st minute.

Southall was similarly embarrassed three minutes later when Kenny Dalglish's pass across his goalmouth was allowed to reach Mark Lawrenson who scored at the far post.

Rush added his third after taking another cunning Dalglish pass clear of Everton's cover by virtue of being first to the ball when his initial shot rebounded from the foot of a post.

The Welshman's fourth, from a raking through ball by Alan Hansen bore a telling similarity to his first again created by Hansen's eye for the opening through the middle.

A measure of the "shambles" manager Howard Kendall described as his defence, was the ration of four unopposed runs that Rush was allowed on Southall's goal.

Only the woodwork denied Rush a 100 per cent striking rate

And while Rush took home the champagne and the match ball, there was an equally significant performance from Sammy Lee, who simply worked his socks off in Liverpool's cause.

EVERTON: Southall, Borrows, Bailey, Keeley, Wright, McMahon, Heath, Johnson, Sharp, King, Sheedy. Sub: Richardson 74 minutes for Johnson.
LIVERPOOL: Grobbelaar, Neal, Kennedy, Thompson, Johnston, Hansen, Dalglish, Lee, Rush, Lawrenson, Souness. Sub Hodgson (82 minutes for Dalglish).
REFEREE: Mr Derek Civil of Birmingham.
ATTENDANCE: 52,741. RECEIPTS: £125,500.

Rush again—this time with the second goal.

Easy . . . Ian Rush put in his fourth and Liverpool's fifth.

Ian Rush cracks in a shot which rebounds off the post—but with Bailey stranded he gets the rebound and slams it in for the fourth goal.

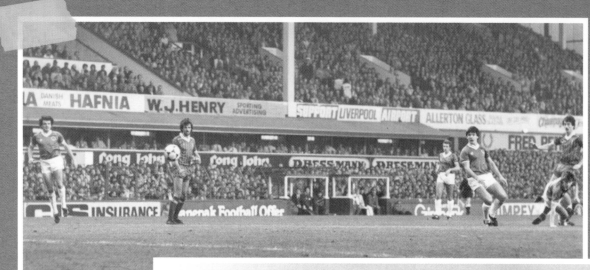

Four Goals But Nev Was Great!

Bob Paisley had taken me to one side beforehand and told me that no-one had scored a hat-trick in the derby for 40 or 50 years.

He may have just been trying to fire me up but part of me thinks, Bob being Bob, he had spotted something in the way Everton set up that made him believe I could get at them a bit. But I don't think even he could have predicted what followed.

It was just one of those games when you feel you can score with every attack and I was lucky enough to get the four goals and Mark Lawrenson got the other.

What a lot of people don't remember, though, is Neville Southall was absolutely brilliant that day. He made some unbelievable saves and without him we probably would have scored even more.

'I love that the supporters still sing about those goals. There are lads singing it who probably didn't even see me play, so generations have passed the song down. That's a great feeling'

Poor Scouser Tommy

Let me tell you the story of a poor boy,
Who was sent far away from his home,
To fight for his king and his country,
And also the old folks back home.

So they put him in a higher division,
Sent him off to a far foreign land,
Where the flies swarm around in their thousands,
And there's nothing to see but the sand.

Now the battle it started next morning,
Under the radiant sun,
I remember our poor Scouser Tommy,
He was shot by an old Nazi gun.

As he lay on the battlefield dying-dying-dying,
With the blood gushing out of his head (out of his head)
As he lay on the battlefield dying-dying-dying,
These were the last words he said:

0hhh, I am a Liverpudlian,
and I come from the Spion Kop,
I like to sing, I like to chant,
I go there quite a lot.

Support a team, that plays in red,
A team that we all know,
A team that we call Liverpool,
To glory we will go.

We won the league, we won the cup,
We've been to Europe too,
We played the Toffees for a laugh,
And left them feeling blue (5-0)

1-2, 1-2-3, 1-2-3-4, 5-0!

Rush scored one, Rush scored two,
Rush scored three, And Rush scored four...

IAN RUSH HITS A HAT-FULL

Liverpool 6, Luton 0.

LIVERPOOL destroyed Luton with an avalanche of goals at Anfield this afternoon, Ian Rush hitting five and Kenny Dalglish also joining in the champions super-show.

Scoring Five Against Luton...But I Wanted Six!

29.10.83

One of my ambitions was to hit six goals in the space of 90 minutes. I came close against Luton, scoring five in a 6-0 win at Anfield.

I'd missed the game against Brentford in the Milk Cup earlier in the week with a groin virus, but I got off to a flying start and after about 75 seconds, the ball dropped to me in the box and I hit it home from close range.

Within a few minutes, I'd scored again. Sammy Lee and Kenny worked a short free-kick and Dalglish chipped in a perfect centre. Souness came flying in and hit the bar with a powerful header, and I knocked in the rebound.

My hat-trick was a decent header after Steve Nicol had whipped in a pin-point cross from the left byline.

I remember hitting a stunning volley for my fourth goal in the second half which was the pick of the bunch. Alan Kennedy floated in a long ball and I met it full-on with my right foot.

I got my fifth and made it 6-0 with a few minutes to go, mopping up on another attempt from Souness which the keeper, Les Sealey, had blocked.

Looking back, I had a few more chances in the game to get my double hat-trick and I'm sure I even had one ruled out for offside, but I suppose you can't really complain when you've just scored five.

And I Wasn't The Only One...

Hard to believe it, but I wasn't the only striker to score five goals in the First Division on October 29, 1983.

Tony Woodcock also managed it on the same day for Arsenal in a 6-2 win over Aston Villa – a post-war record for the Gunners.

Heading Through In Spain

02.11.83

**v Athletic Bilbao, San Mames,
European Cup, 2nd Rnd, 2nd Leg**

After a goalless first leg at Anfield, my header
managed to settle this second round European tie in
our favour. With 25 minutes left, I latched on to a cross
from Alan Kennedy and powered home a header that
left goalkeeper Andoni Zubizarreta with no chance.

Mirror Sport

Saturday, January 21, 1984 No. 24,857
Telephone: (STD Code 01) - 353 0246
CHANNEL ISLANDS 17p

Clough's £250,000 bonanza

Forest boss gets a pay rise but he'll cut players' cash

By DAVID MOORE

BRIAN CLOUGH has signed a lucrative new contract, probably worth £250,000 plus bonuses, which will keep him at Nottingham Forest until the summer of 1988.

And chairman Maurice Roworth revealed last night that Forest are already planning moves designed to convince their brilliant manager he should stick around even longer.

Roworth, whose election in October ahead of former vice-chairman Fred Reacher—Clough's closest boardroom ally—sparked City Ground controversy, stated: "Everyone is delighted about Brian putting pen to paper.

"It's a great day for the club, because we all regard him as the best boss in football, bar none. The next step is obvious. Forest must try to ensure that hopes of Brian staying here after this contract ends are turned into reality."

Clough has cheerfully accepted a basic salary increase to £65,000 per annum, despite being absolutely determined that Forest's wage bill, with several players facing big pay cuts.

He admitted: "At the moment I'm feeling quite content.

"I've said it before, and I'll say it again. Forest will definitely be my last management post. Another two-and-a-half years suits me fine right now, and I'll throw everything into the job.

"Forest still possess bags of potential and I hope we can win further honours."

Liverpool hit man fires three to put skids under Villa

ICE-BREAKER RUSH

By DAVE HORRIDGE: Aston Villa 1, Liverpool 3

IAN RUSH added live television's first hat trick to his remarkable scoring achievements for Liverpool last night.

The Welsh striker took his season's total for the club to 27 in a game in which they outclassed Aston Villa and put themselves two points clear at the top of the First Division.

The crowd of 19,586 was 15,000 below Villa's estimate of the gates drawing power if it hadn't been going into millions of living rooms. They will be claiming nearly £40,000 compensation—the biggest so far in the nine-match TV series.

Rush equalised in the opening minute of the second half when he ran onto a long clearance by

DENNIS MORTIMER Puts Villa ahead—but not for long.   Picture: DICK WILLIAMS

Mark Lawrenson, held off a challenge by Gary Williams and pushed the ball past Nigel Spink.

His second, 26 minutes later in a certainty for action replay. Steve Nicol touched on a cross by Graeme Souness and Rush met the ball on the volley and it screamed into the far corner of the net.

Nine minutes from time, Rush cashed in on a mistake by Allan Evans and coolly lobbed in his third.

Within seconds of the kick-off it was clear that the conditions were more suited to the champions Torvill and Dean than footballers.

Peter Withe demonstrated the problems of the frosty conditions when, in trying to shoot on the turn he couldn't get his feet in position and sent the ball yards wide.

The Motorin', Huntin', Fishin', Workin', GALE COAT MADE IN ENGLAND

You don't so much slip into it as snuggle into it. Even in a torrential downpour and gale force winds it will keep you dry and cocoon you in warmth and luxury. Which is why we call it the Gale Coat.

LUXURY LINING. Made from very lightweight, very tough, specially coated cloth in 100% nylon and lined with luxurious synthetic fur fabric. The collar is trimmed with corduroy for extra warmth and comfort.

LOTS OF EXTRA PROTECTION. There's a fly front to provide additional protection from the wind; a lined detachable hood; side pockets with hand-warmer pockets. Inside security pocket; heavy duty zip opening top and bottom; storm cuffs.

At £28.75 incl. VAT, it has to be the biggest bargain of the winter.

Colours: Beige, 36", 38", 40", 42", 44", 46".

ONLY £28.75
AND £3 P+P FOR EACH COAT

BOYCOTT ROW CRUNCH DAY

By HOWARD BOOTH

GEOFF BOYCOTT'S supporters plan to continue their fight against the Headingley Establishment—win or lose today.

A packed house at the Harrogate conference centre will know by 2 p.m. whether the 43-year-old batsman has been reinstated and whether the club's government has been brought down.

But whatever the voting the Yorkshire 1984 Group will soldier on. Their chairman Peter Briggs said yesterday:

"Even if we are beaten on all three resolutions it will not be the end for us. The district elections are due next month and we have six candidates for seats on the general committee.

"The whole thing was started with the sacking of Geoffrey Boycott. Members want to see him back but the argument is about how the club is being managed. The men responsible for that are not doing it properly."

BOYCOTT: D-day

Printed and Published by THE DAILY MIRROR NEWSPAPERS LTD., at and for, Mirror Group Newspapers Ltd., Holborn Circus, London, EC1P 1DQ. Registered at the Post Office as a newspaper.

The First Live TV Hat-trick (And I Did It On An Ice-rink)

20.01.84

v Aston Villa, Villa Park, Football League Division One

1. A long punt forward from the back dropped beyond the Villa defence and I used my pace to get to the ball first and hit it low beyond Nigel Spink.

2. Graeme Souness delivered a cross from the right, Steve Nicol couldn't quite control the ball but flicked it on and I smashed a left-foot volley home from the left-hand side of the box. It was probably the best of the three technique-wise.

3. With 10 minutes left, I found some space in the box and managed to lob Spink from 12 yards to cap off a wonderful Friday night.

My goals as they happened. Liverpool boss Joe Fagan later came up with the famous phrase that I had scored 'a hat-trick on an ice-rink'

57

Rome Here We Come...

25.04.84

**v Dinamo Bucharest,
23 August Stadium,
European Cup,
Semi-final, 2nd Leg**

My first goal in this match saw me collect the ball close to the edge of the box before swivelling onto my left foot and dinking over the onrushing Dinamo keeper, Dumitru Moraru.

Nothing beats scoring the winning goal – especially in a game as important as a European Cup semi-final – and with six minutes to play, Ronnie Whelan's cross wasn't cleared by the Dinamo defence and that allowed me to pounce and strike home the winner.

A Couple Of Special Goals

25.02.84

**v QPR, Anfield,
Football League Division One**

I had just signed a new four-year contract and celebrated with a long-range effort from outside the box – a collector's item!

18.04.84

**v Leicester City, Filbert Street,
Football League Division One**

It was a decent game which ended 3-3. I scored after an hour to make it 2-2, beating Tommy Williams inside the area before poking home. A nice way to bring up my 100th Reds goal.

30.05.84

v Roma, Stadio Olimpico, European Cup Final

This doesn't officially count as one of my 346 LFC goals, but I was really nervous walking up to take my spot-kick. Thankfully I managed to send the goalkeeper the wrong way. Afterwards, I put my hand to my chest to check my heart was still there!

'I put my hand to my chest to check my heart was still there!'

Last-gasp Goal Spurs Us On

02.03.86

v Tottenham Hotspur, Anfield, Football League Division One

Sometimes it only takes one result to really ignite a season, and this last minute 2-1 win was definitely one of those games – especially because it was me who scored that last-gasp goal! As the clock ticked down, Ronnie Whelan produced an inch-perfect pass and I beat Ray Clemence to thankfully get all three points.

Extra-time Winner On Road To Wembley

17.03.86

v Watford, Vicarage Road, FA Cup, 6th Rnd Replay

We had been a goal down and looking at defeat after John Barnes (whatever happened to him?) had opened the scoring for Watford. I won us a penalty which Jan Molby converted before I won the game in extra-time with a left-footed strike into the bottom corner.

'Sometimes it only takes one result to really ignite a season, and this last minute 2-1 win was one of those games'

Another Euro Treble

24.10.84

v Benfica, Anfield, European Cup, 2nd Rnd, 1st Leg

A rainy night at Anfield, but that was soon forgotten as I scored a hat-trick. I tapped in from close range for number one. A Ronnie Whelan shot crossed my path for number two – and I never missed the opportunity to get the final touch! I scored my third with 15 minutes to go, thanks to Ronnie again. A deep cross from Craig Johnston found Whelan, and after his shot was blocked, the ball fell to me and I poked in once again.

Goal That Turned Cup Final Back In Our Favour

10.05.86

v Everton, Wembley, FA Cup Final

Nothing beats scoring at Wembley – or against Everton! Jan Molby was the provider as I skipped through Everton's defence, rounded Bobby Mimms and slotted home to make it 1-1 after Gary Lineker had put them in front in the first half. I was delighted – even if Craig Johnston slid in to try and nab the last touch.

Double At Wembley Is Twice As Nice

10.05.86

v Everton, Wembley, FA Cup Final

Only one thing beats scoring once at Wembley – and that's scoring twice!

We were already 2-1 up when Ronnie Whelan chipped the ball through and I hit it nice and early to seal the League and FA Cup double...and smash a camera behind the goal in the process.

Opening Up The Home Guard

23.08.86

v Newcastle, St James' Park, Football League Division One

It was always nice to 'nutmeg' a keeper and this time was no different. I ran half the length of the pitch and slotted through the legs of Martin Thomas to give us the lead.

Perfect Finish To A Tyneside Triumph

23.08.86

v Newcastle, St James' Park, Football League Division One

A great game for me and the Reds then became better as I fired into the top corner with seven minutes to go to seal the 2-0 win.

Volley Brings Up Double Century

18.03.87

v QPR, Anfield, Football League Division One

This goal helped me pass another milestone as it was my 200th strike for the Reds from just 321 games. Mark Lawrenson and Craig Johnston combined to set Barry Venison off down the right wing and I volleyed home his cross to bring up my double century.

First Blemish On My Goalscoring Record

05.04.87

v Arsenal, Wembley League Cup Final

This was the first game in my Liverpool career that we lost after I had scored. Not a bad record after almost six years at the club! Steve McMahon played me in and I slipped the ball under the onrushing John Lukic with my right foot.

Final Derby Contribution Before Heading For Italy

25.04.87

Everton, Anfield, Football League Division One

Gary Ablett's cross from the left beat Everton's Kevin Ratcliffe which allowed me to poke past Neville Southall.

It was nice to score in my last Merseyside derby before my move to Juventus.

Close Range Finish Ends First Stint With The Reds

09.05.87

Chelsea, Stamford Bridge, Football League Division One

I grabbed my 40th goal of the season to end on a high note ahead of my move to Juventus.

John Aldridge played a neat ball square across the box and I happily tapped in from close range.

Goals By Season (up to 1987)

1981/82

Date	Opposition	H/A	Competition	Result
1) 30/09/81	Oulu Palloseura	H	European Cup	7-0
2) 07/10/81	Exeter City	H	League Cup	5-0
3) 07/10/81	Exeter City	H	League Cup	5-0
4) 10/10/81	Leeds United	H	Division One	3-0
5) 10/10/81	Leeds United	H	Division One	3-0
6) 28/10/81	Exeter City	A	League Cup	6-0
7) 28/10/81	Exeter City	A	League Cup	6-0
8) 04/11/81	AZ Alkmaar	H	European Cup	3-2
9) 07/11/81	Everton	H	Division One	3-1
10) 10/11/81	Middlesbrough	H	League Cup	4-1
11) 02/01/82	Swansea City	A	FA Cup	4-0
12) 02/01/82	Swansea City	A	FA Cup	4-0
13) 23/01/81	Sunderland	A	FA Cup	3-0
14) 26/01/82	Notts County	A	Division One	4-0
15) 26/01/82	Notts County	A	Division One	4-0
16) 26/01/82	Notts County	A	Division One	4-0
17) 30/01/82	Aston Villa	A	Division One	3-0
18) 02/02/82	Ipswich Town	A	League Cup	2-0
19) 06/02/82	Ipswich Town	H	Division One	4-0
20) 09/02/82	Ipswich Town	H	League Cup	2-2
21) 20/02/82	Coventry City	H	Division One	4-0
22) 27/02/82	Leeds United	A	Division One	2-0
23) 13/03/82	Tottenham Hotspur	N	League Cup	3-1
24) 20/03/82	Sunderland	H	Division One	1-0
25) 30/03/82	Birmingham City	H	Division One	3-1
26) 30/03/82	Birmingham City	H	Division One	3-1
27) 10/04/82	Manchester City	A	Division One	5-0
28) 24/04/82	Southampton	A	Division One	3-2
29) 08/05/82	Birmingham City	A	Division One	1-0
30) 11/05/82	Arsenal	A	Division One	1-1

1982/83

Date	Opposition	H/A	Competition	Result
31) 21/08/82	Tottenham Hotspur	N	Charity Shield	1-0
32) 07/09/82	Nottingham Forest	H	Division One	4-3
33) 11/09/82	Luton Town	H	Division One	3-3
34) 14/09/82	Dundalk	A	European Cup	4-1
35) 18/09/92	Swansea City	A	Division One	3-0
36) 18/09/92	Swansea City	A	Division One	3-0
37) 05/10/82	Ipswich Town	A	League Cup	2-1
38) 05/10/82	Ipswich Town	A	League Cup	2-1
39) 06/11/82	Everton	A	Division One	5-0
40) 06/11/82	Everton	A	Division One	5-0
41) 06/11/82	Everton	A	Division One	5-0
42) 06/11/82	Everton	A	Division One	5-0
43) 13/11/82	Coventry City	H	Division One	4-0
44) 13/11/82	Coventry City	H	Division One	4-0
45) 13/11/82	Coventry City	H	Division One	4-0
46) 11/12/82	Watford	H	Division One	3-1
47) 18/12/82	Aston Villa	A	Division One	4-2
48) 27/12/82	Manchester City	H	Division One	5-2
49) 01/01/83	Notts County	H	Division One	5-1
50) 01/01/83	Notts County	H	Division One	5-1
51) 01/01/83	Notts County	H	Division One	5-1
52) 03/01/83	Arsenal	H	Division One	3-1
53) 08/01/83	Blackburn Rovers	A	FA Cup	2-1
54) 15/01/83	WBA	A	Division One	1-0
55) 29/01/83	Stoke City	H	FA Cup	2-0
56) 05/02/83	Luton Town	A	Division One	3-1
57) 13/03/83	West Ham United	H	Division One	3-0
58) 16/03/83	Widzew Lodz	H	European Cup	3-2
59) 22/03/83	Brighton	A	Division One	2-2
60) 22/03/83	Brighton	A	Division One	2-2
61) 09/04/83	Swansea City	H	Division One	3-0

1983/84

Date	Opposition	H/A	Competition	Result
62) 27/08/83	Wolves	A	Division One	1-1
63) 03/09/83	Nottingham Forest	H	Division One	1-0
64) 06/09/83	Southampton	H	Division One	1-1
65) 17/09/83	Aston Villa	H	Division One	2-1
66) 05/10/83	Brentford	A	League Cup	4-1
67) 05/10/83	Brentford	A	League Cup	4-1
68) 29/10/83	Luton Town	H	Division One	6-0
69) 29/10/83	Luton Town	H	Division One	6-0
70) 29/10/83	Luton Town	H	Division One	6-0
71) 29/10/83	Luton Town	H	Division One	6-0
72) 29/10/83	Luton Town	H	Division One	6-0
73) 02/11/83	Athletic Bilbao	A	European Cup	1-0
74) 06/11/83	Everton	H	Division One	3-0
75) 08/11/83	Fulham	A	League Cup	1-1
76) 12/11/83	Tottenham Hotspur	A	Division One	2-2
77) 19/11/83	Stoke City	H	Division One	1-0
78) 03/12/83	Birmingham City	H	Division One	1-0
79) 17/12/83	Notts County	H	Division One	5-0
80) 22/12/83	Birmingham City	H	League Cup	3-0
81) 22/12/83	Birmingham City	H	League Cup	3-0
82) 27/12/83	Leicester City	H	Division One	2-2
83) 31/12/83	Nottingham Forest	A	Division One	1-0
84) 06/01/84	Newcastle United	H	FA Cup	4-0
85) 06/01/84	Newcastle United	H	FA Cup	4-0
86) 20/01/84	Aston Villa	A	Division One	3-1
87) 20/01/84	Aston Villa	A	Division One	3-1
88) 20/01/84	Aston Villa	A	Division One	3-1
89) 25/01/84	Sheffield Wednesday	H	League Cup	3-0
90) 25/01/84	Sheffield Wednesday	H	League Cup	3-0
91) 01/02/84	Watford	H	Division One	3-0
92) 14/02/84	Walsall	A	League Cup	2-0
93) 25/02/84	QPR	H	Division One	2-0
94) 03/03/84	Everton	A	Division One	1-1
95) 07/03/84	Benfica	H	European Cup	1-0
96) 21/03/84	Benfica	A	European Cup	4-1
97) 31/03/84	Watford	A	Division One	2-0
98) 07/04/84	West Ham United	H	Division One	6-0
99) 07/04/84	West Ham United	H	Division One	6-0
100) 18/04/84	Leicester City	A	Division One	3-3
101) 25/04/84	Dinamo Bucharest	A	European Cup	2-1
102) 25/04/84	Dinamo Bucharest	A	European Cup	2-1
103) 28/04/84	Ipswich Town	H	Division One	2-2
104) 07/05/84	Coventry City	H	Division One	5-0
105) 07/05/84	Coventry City	H	Division One	5-0
106) 07/05/84	Coventry City	H	Division One	5-0
107) 07/05/84	Coventry Cit y	H	Division One	5-0
108) 15/05/84	Norwich City	H	Division One	1-1

When I Scored...

Period	Total
1-15 mins	44
16-30 mins	45
31-45 mins	38
46-60 mins	58
61-75 mins	68
76-90 mins	86
91-120 mins	7

	Date	Opposition	H/A	Competition	Result
152)	21/01/86	Ipswich Town	H	League Cup	3-0
153)	26/01/86	Chelsea	A	FA Cup	2-1
154)	02/03/86	Tottenham Hotspur	A	Division One	2-1
155)	08/03/86	QPR	H	Division One	4-1
156)	15/03/86	Southampton	A	Division One	2-1
157)	17/03/86	Watford	A	FA Cup	2-1
158)	22/03/86	Oxford United	H	Division One	6-0
159)	22/03/86	Oxford United	H	Division One	6-0
160)	05/04/86	Southampton	N	FA Cup	2-0
161)	05/04/86	Southampton	N	FA Cup	2-0
162)	12/04/86	Coventry City	H	Division One	5-0
163)	19/04/86	WBA	A	Division One	2-1
164)	26/04/86	Birmingham City	H	Division One	5-0
165)	30/04/86	Leicester City	A	Division One	2-0
166)	10/05/86	Everton	N	FA Cup	3-1
167)	10/05/86	Everton	N	FA Cup	3-1

1984/85

	Date	Opposition	H/A	Competition	Result
109)	24/10/85	Benfica	H	European Cup	3-1
110)	24/10/85	Benfica	H	European Cup	3-1
111)	24/10/85	Benfica	H	European Cup	3-1
112)	28/10/84	Nottingham Forest	A	Division One	2-0
113)	10/11/84	Southampton	H	Division One	1-1
114)	04/12/84	Coventry City	H	Division One	3-1
115)	21/12/84	QPR	A	Division One	3-1
116)	01/01/85	Watford	A	Division One	1-1
117)	05/01/85	Aston Villa	H	FA Cup	3-0
118)	05/01/85	Aston Villa	H	FA Cup	3-0
119)	19/01/85	Norwich City	H	Division One	4-0
120)	19/01/85	Norwich City	H	Division One	4-0
121)	27/01/85	Tottenham Hotspur	H	FA Cup	1-0
122)	12/02/85	Arsenal	H	Division One	3-0
123)	16/02/85	York City	A	FA Cup	1-1
124)	10/03/85	Barnsley	A	FA Cup	4-0
125)	10/03/85	Barnsley	A	FA Cup	4-0
126)	10/03/85	Barnsley	A	FA Cup	4-0
127)	03/04/85	Sunderland	A	Division One	3-0
128)	03/04/85	Sunderland	A	Division One	3-0
129)	10/04/85	Panathinaikos	H	European Cup	4-0
130)	10/04/85	Panathinaikos	H	European Cup	4-0
131)	04/05/85	Chelsea	H	Division One	4-3
132)	11/05/85	Aston Villa	H	Division One	2-1
133)	17/05/85	Watford	H	Division One	4-3
134)	17/05/85	Watford	H	Division One	4-3

1986/87

	Date	Opposition	H/A	Competition	Result
168)	16/08/86	Everton	N	Charity Shield	1-1
169)	23/08/86	Newcastle United	A	Division One	2-0
170)	23/08/86	Newcastle United	A	Division One	2-0
171)	30/08/86	Arsenal	H	Division One	2-1
172)	06/09/86	West Ham United	A	Division One	5-2
173)	13/09/86	Charlton Athletic	H	Division One	2-0
174)	16/09/86	Everton	H	Scr Sp Super Cup	3-1
175)	16/09/86	Everton	H	Scr Sp Super Cup	3-1
176)	23/09/86	Fulham	H	League Cup	10-0
177)	23/09/86	Fulham	H	League Cup	10-0
178)	30/09/86	Everton	A	Scr Sp Super Cup	4-1
179)	30/09/86	Everton	A	Scr Sp Super Cup	4-1
180)	30/09/86	Everton	A	Scr Sp Super Cup	4-1
181)	04/10/86	Wimbledon	A	Division One	3-1
182)	04/10/86	Wimbledon	A	Division One	3-1
183)	18/10/86	Oxford United	H	Division One	4-0
184)	18/10/86	Oxford United	H	Division One	4-0
185)	01/11/86	Norwich City	H	Division One	6-2
186)	01/11/86	Norwich City	H	Division One	6-2
187)	08/11/86	QPR	A	Division One	3-1
188)	16/11/86	Sheffield Wednesday	H	Division One	1-1
189)	14/12/86	Chelsea	H	Division One	3-0
190)	27/12/86	Sheffield Wednesday	A	Division One	1-0
191)	01/01/87	Nottingham Forest	A	Division One	1-1
192)	17/01/87	Manchester City	A	Division One	1-0
193)	21/01/87	Everton	A	League Cup	1-0
194)	24/01/87	Newcastle United	H	Division One	2-0
195)	14/02/87	Leicester City	H	Division One	4-3
196)	14/02/87	Leicester City	H	Division One	4-3
197)	14/02/87	Leicester City	H	Division One	4-3
198)	10/03/87	Arsenal	A	Division One	1-0
199)	14/03/87	Oxford United	A	Division One	3-1
200)	18/03/87	QPR	H	Division One	2-1
201)	18/03/87	QPR	H	Division One	2-1
202)	05/04/87	Arsenal	N	League Cup	1-2
203)	11/04/87	Norwich City	A	Division One	1-2
204)	25/04/87	Everton	H	Division One	3-1
205)	25/04/87	Everton	H	Division One	3-1
206)	04/05/87	Watford	H	Division One	1-0
207)	09/05/87	Chelsea	A	Division One	3-3

1985/86

	Date	Opposition	H/A	Competition	Result
135)	21/08/85	Aston Villa	A	Division One	2-2
136)	26/08/85	Ipswich Town	H	Division One	5-0
137)	26/08/85	Ipswich Town	H	Division One	5-0
138)	07/09/85	Watford	H	Division One	3-1
139)	14/09/85	Oxford United	A	Division One	2-2
140)	21/09/85	Everton	A	Division One	3-2
141)	24/09/85	Oldham Athletic	H	League Cup	3-0
142)	28/09/85	Tottenham Hotspur	H	Division One	4-1
143)	09/10/85	Oldham Athletic	A	League Cup	5-2
144)	02/11/85	Leicester City	H	Division One	1-0
145)	09/11/85	Coventry City	A	Division One	3-0
146)	23/11/85	Birmingham City	A	Division One	2-0
147)	01/01/86	Sheffield Wednesday	H	Division One	2-2
148)	12/01/86	Watford	A	Division One	3-2
149)	14/01/86	Tottenham Hotspur	A	Scr Sp Super Cup	3-0
150)	14/01/86	Tottenham Hotspur	A	Scr Sp Super Cup	3-0
151)	18/01/86	West Ham United	H	Division One	3-1

• Liverpool score shown first

GOALKEEPERS. THE BAD NEWS IS HE WEARS NIKE. THERE

ON THE BALL

From kicking any old ball on the streets and school field, to kicking an adidas Tango in the European Cup final and sticking a Mitre in the net at Wembley. My memories of having a ball...

WEMBLEY SPECIAL

The big crunch

Ian wants to leave in a

You've Been Tangoed

When I was at Liverpool, the adidas Tango was the ball that sticks out in my mind. We used to play with the Tango balls every week at Anfield and we loved them. We trained with them every day and we found that we could ping them far more easily than the Mitre balls of the time, which helped our passing game.

Other clubs got on to this and it was amazing how often that, when we went away from home, we'd be up against sides who would use Mitre balls instead to try and stop us from playing. It happened a lot in the early 1980s. The Tango balls moved a lot quicker and they really suited the players we had at Liverpool. Opponents wanted to slow us down and the Mitre ball was a lot heavier, so they'd use them.

Plastic Ball And Pitch

Slipping and sliding on Luton's artificial pitch at Kenilworth Road during the FA Cup third round match which ended 0-0

Wacky Wembley Ball

Another one that stands out, funnily enough, was the Mitre Surridge ball which I think we played with in the 1982 League Cup final. It had red patches on it and I think that was the start of how things are now in terms of making footballs a commercial thing for people to buy.

Memories Of Jumpers For Goalposts And Lampposts For Target Practice

When we were kids we'd just play in the streets with any football we could get our hands on. Any make, any colour, whatever. There weren't as many cars around back then so we'd play in the streets, but kids can't do that now.

There was one game we used to play when you had to aim for the lamppost. You had three lives and you'd lose one every time you missed it. When we were lucky enough to get on grass, we'd be playing football all day.

Hat-trick BALLS

v Everton
06.11.1982

I've already relived the goals from the famous derby of 1982 when we beat Everton 5-0 at Goodison Park – and this is the ball from that game.

Bob Paisley actually said to me before the game that I was going to score a hat-trick, which was something coming from the great man himself.

I got the ball to keep after the match, but a lot of the signatures have wiped off over the years.

On the Monday after the game I asked Kevin Ratcliffe, who wasn't playing that night, could he go into training and get the Everton players to sign the ball for me.

I'm not going to say in this scrapbook what he actually said back to me, but he reluctantly took it into training and got them to sign it.

What he didn't tell them, until after they'd signed it, was what the ball was and who they were signing it for! He said if they'd have known, they wouldn't have signed it.

It was a great feeling scoring four goals against Everton. It was a dream come true, especially as I used to support them, and something that I'll always remember because Liverpool fans love to comment on that game!

This is my matchball from the 4-0 win over Notts County in 1982. All three of my goals that day came in the second half, with Ronnie Whelan the other goalscorer.

'Watch out Maradona' was the advice written on this hat-trick ball from one of my team-mates.

Among the words of congratulations on this adidas ball was the less flattering inscription 'Lucky again!'

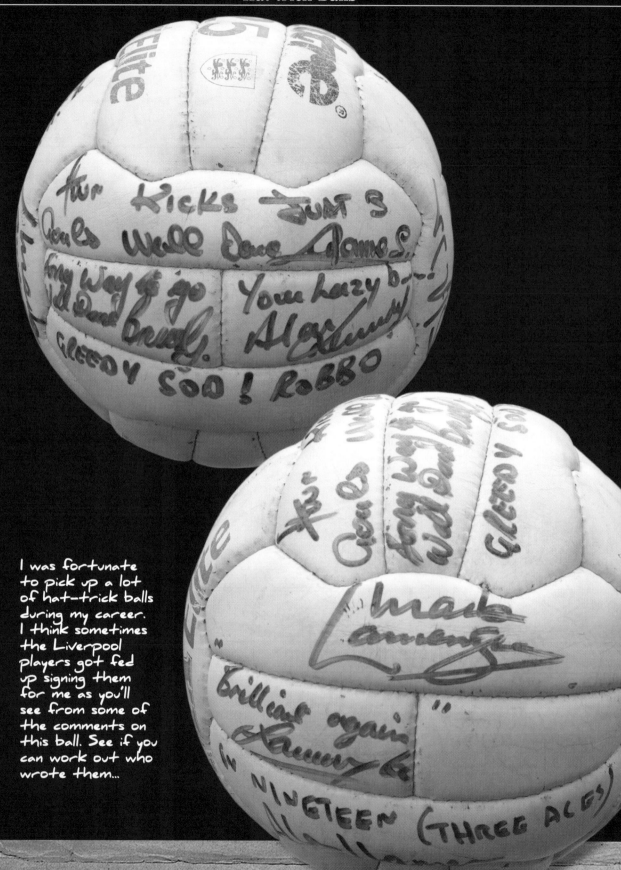

I was fortunate to pick up a lot of hat-trick balls during my career. I think sometimes the Liverpool players got fed up signing them for me as you'll see from some of the comments on this ball. See if you can work out who wrote them...

My
PHOTO ALBUM

From triumphant highs to emotional goodbyes, it seems like the camera has always been there to capture my special moments. Here are some selected pictures you may not have seen including a few snapshots from my personal collection

One of the family: To mark my final season at Liverpool before moving to Juventus, we posed for a Rush family picture at my mum and dad's in Flint. The Rush clan are: Back: Doris (mum), Graham, Gerald, Peter, Francis, Steven, Francis (dad). Front: Janet, Pauline, me, Carol, Susan

Night of legends: With Anfield heroes Kenny Dalglish, Ray Clemence, Tommy Smith and John Barnes at a dinner to celebrate the Football League's Centenary at the Hilton Hotel in London

Trophy time: Bringing the 1983 Milk Cup on to the Anfield pitch with Phil Thompson

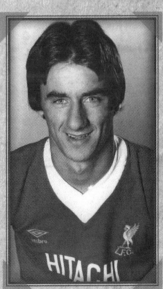

New boy: One of the first images of me in my LFC kit

Strike partner: People used to say me and John Aldridge couldn't play up front together, but if you look at the records, at least one of us scored pretty much every time we did. I enjoyed playing alongside Aldo and this picture was taken during a 2-2 draw at Newcastle in February 1989. Liverpool's goalscorers that day? Rush and Aldridge

By royal appointment: I was proud to visit Buckingham Palace with Tracey, Jonathan and Daniel to collect an MBE from the Queen in 1996

The cap doesn't quite fit: Daniel was just five weeks old when this picture was taken in 1993, but I was already making sure his allegiances lay with Wales, just like my dad did with me when I was a kid

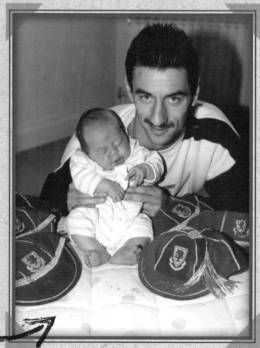

Prize guy: There were plenty of pictures and plates among my fair share of awards

Sitting on top of the world: Recording our 1986 FA Cup final song; our voices were slightly better than the fashion on show!

Liver-fooling around: The boys always had a great time at the fancy dress Christmas party and it was no surprise that Bruce Grobbelaar turned up to this one as the Joker from Batman. The less said about David Burrows' outfit the better!

Letting my guard down: This isn't a Liverpool strip from the 1980s but the Beefeater outfit I wore for one of the legendary club Christmas do's. I'm not entirely sure what I was singing here, but I don't think I'd have won X-Factor had it been around back then!

Wishing for success:
Me and Ronnie Whelan
ahead of another
Wembley final

On the pull: Leicester
try to keep me quiet
by resorting to some
shirt pulling in 1985

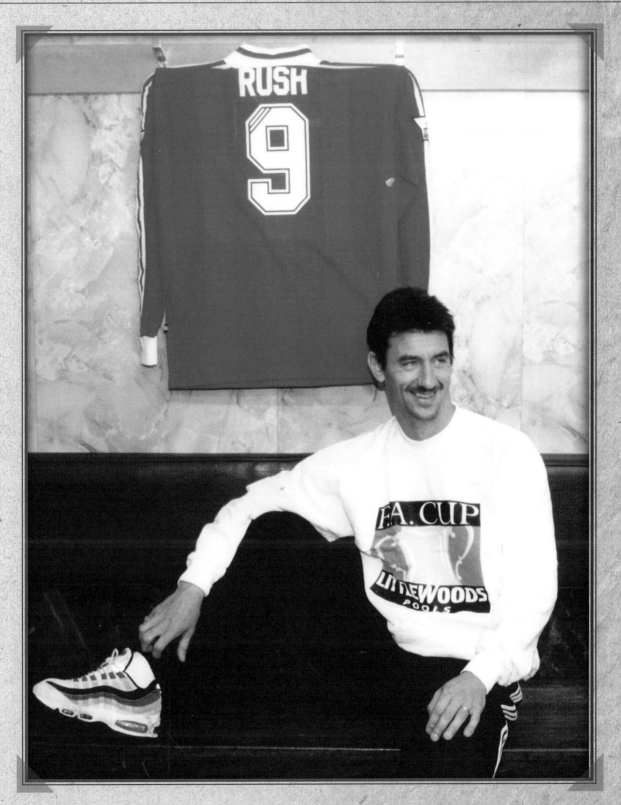

Catalogue pose: Trying to keep a staight face during a photoshoot

On the spot: I didn't
take many penalties
but here I am scoring in
the FA Cup semi-final
replay shoot-out against
Portsmouth in 1992

Country folk: Taking a breather
along with Mark Hughes during
training for Wales

It's a great feeling touring the city
with a trophy. This is me after we
won the FA Cup final in '92

ROYAL

Derby duel: Kevin Ratcliffe loved me when I had a Wales shirt on, but wasn't so keen when I was scoring goals against Everton

Waxwork of art: The real thing was much more difficult to mark than the model

Who led the Reds out: I captained Liverpool from 1993 to 1996 and was proud to skipper the club for the last Merseyside derby in front of the old standing Spion Kop. I also got the last of my 25 Merseyside derby goals that day, although the Sky cameras were still showing a replay of Dave Watson's goal when I equalised just a few seconds after the restart!

Santa dash: I had my red santa suit on to take
part in a charity Santa race around Liverpool

Sad day: Returning the applause at Anfield alongside my son in what would be my final league appearance for the Reds

Back of the net: Celebrating with Kenny Dalglish as we equalise against Spurs in 1982

Ian Rush-ia: Liverpool drew Spartak Vladikavkaz in the UEFA Cup in 1995 so I prepared for the chilly temperatures with a bit of extra headwear. I think John Barnes used to wear one of those hats with his tights and gloves every winter!

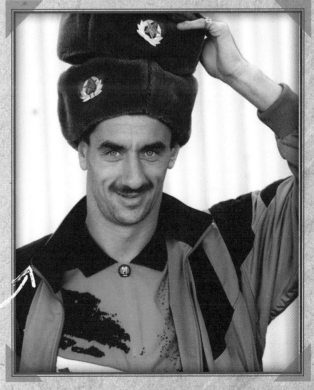

INSIDE THE DRESSING ROOM

I got to know a few Liverpool dressing rooms over the years. Pre-match routines, superstitions and mickey-takes... I saw them all. Step inside and I'll tell you a few secrets about my team-mates and managers

My Pre-Match Routine

For home games, I used to stay in a hotel on a Friday night because I liked my sleep. I'd drive to the hotel at about 8.30pm, check in, have a sandwich and a cup of tea at about 9 o'clock and then go to sleep.

I wouldn't wake up until 10.30 the next morning and then at 11.30am the players would meet at the hotel for a pre-match meal. I'd be ready, having had a good sleep, and I'd have steak, baked beans and toast. You wouldn't get away with eating that today! I'd wash that down with a pint of milk.

After that I'd go for a shower, get changed and we'd leave to go to the game, if it was a 3 o'clock kick-off, at 1.15pm. We'd get a coach to Anfield and be there for 1.45pm.

Then it was a case of sorting your tickets out. Some players used to go out and do the warm-up, but it was only in the last three or four seasons that I started doing that. I preferred to do my warm-up inside.

In terms of superstitions, I always liked to put my shorts on last and before we'd go out I used to go into the toilet and say a prayer. I'm Catholic and I would always pray that the team would win and that I would score. No-one ever knew I used to go in there and say a quick prayer.

My only other superstition involved my boots. For some reason, before a game against Luton, they were rock hard, so I wet my boots. I went on to the pitch, we won 6-0 and I scored five. So ever since that game in 1983 I had to wet my boots no matter what and I still do it now. It's become a massive superstition for me.

Brucie Gets Switched On

Bruce Grobbelaar used to have to try and switch the light on and off in the dressing room with the ball before we went onto the pitch and I think we ended up kicking off at about 10 past three some weeks because of it.

He'd only be stood about three yards away, but sometimes he couldn't do it and we'd be like 'come on Bruce, we should be out there by now'.

There was one game at Wimbledon when it was taking him so long to do it that the referee came into the dressing room and made us go onto the pitch.

Bruce still wouldn't go because he couldn't switch the light on even though he had hit the switch about 10 times. It later turned out that Wimbledon manager Bobby Gould knew about his superstition and had the light fixed so it would never come on. Typical Wimbledon! Fortunately we won that game. Then there was Barry Venison who famously said he puts his right boot on before his right sock, despite him having two left feet!

Getting In The Right Frame Of Mind

When I first went to Liverpool I got changed next to Alan Hansen and Ray Clemence before and after training. Later on it was Hansen and John Barnes. Alan had the same spot, whether it was training or a game, and he wouldn't move for anyone.

The atmosphere was really, really relaxed and there was a lot of mickey taking. Alan Hansen would sit there with the programme and then just go out. Me, Steve McMahon, Ronnie Whelan and Jan Molby would pat each other on the side to wish each other luck, but would do it so hard we'd end up hurting each other.

It was all done with a sense of humour, in the right way, but when we got on the pitch we were very serious. It comes back to team spirit.

The Jokers In The Pack

There were so many practical jokes played at the club, I can't remember what the best one was, but the funny stories always involved Steve Nicol.

Steve took size 14 boots and in those days the lads used to bring your boots in to you. Nico put a new pair of boots on, walked around and said 'these size 14s are too tight.'

He gave them to one of the young YTS lads and told him to go and break them in. The lad turned around and said, 'you do know the paper is still in the toes?'

That was Nico for you and these things always happened in front of everyone. He didn't know he was doing it, which is why he was so funny.

He got some Air Mail once and you know how all the writing would be on the envelope? He opened the envelope and told the rest of us some idiot had sent him a letter with nothing in it.

I was with him in Boston on the pre-season tour – he lives out there – and we had a good chat. All we talked about was what happened in the old days in the dressing room. We were laughing our heads off at some of the memories.

The Best Team-mates On A Night Out

We'd go on a night out as a whole group. Steve Nicol would always be the last there, but we'd go out as a group and come back as a group.

Kenny was great to go out with. He has a very dry sense of humour and once Kenny knows you, he can be really funny.

Alan Hansen was funny too, they have a different sense of humour, and with lads like Bruce, Steve Nicol, Ronnie Whelan and Jan there, we had a group of lads who could really enjoy themselves.

The Most Vain Player At Liverpool?

That was Barry Venison, when he was there, and before him, Graeme Souness.

Souey loved looking after himself. People used to say he looks like Terry Mac so they'd try and do their hair differently, but Terry would then take the mick out of Souey and say that they still look the same. You couldn't get Barry Venison away from the mirror though.

Memories Of Bob Paisley

I couldn't understand a lot of what he was saying. He'd say things like 'he's not quick, but he's nippy'. He was quiet, Bob, but he was very knowledgeable and with Joe Fagan, Ronnie Moran – who never stopped shouting – and Roy Evans there, it was a good mix.

Joe was quiet, but when he shouted you knew about it, and Roy was learning the ropes. He was mates with the players, which he had to be because he was around us the most.

One-on-one, Bob was very good, but in front of the team, he found it difficult. The thing was, even though you couldn't understand him, you knew what he was saying. A normal person wouldn't have understood, but the players at Liverpool were so knowledgeable they knew what he meant and what he was trying to say.

We All Took Notice Of Joe Fagan

Joe did two years as manager and he was the opposite to Bob. When we played badly, he'd tell us to get to bed early because we'd be running all next week, but come Monday, we'd do no training at all.

Sometimes he'd say nothing and let Ronnie Moran get on with it, but when he did speak, everyone would take notice, even Graeme Souness and Kenny Dalglish. Joe used to have a go at them more than the likes of me and Ronnie Whelan because we were only 23 or 24. Souey and Kenny were elder statesmen and Joe would give them a right rollicking and tell them it was their job to sort problems out.

They realised, as players, they had to get the dressing room sorted out because Joe would let them know that in no uncertain terms.

Kenny Dalglish 'The Boss'

He took to management really well and the good thing about it was that the likes of Ronnie Moran said to us 'you have to call him boss now, you can't just call him Kenny'. It was strange for a week or two as Kenny would go down to Melwood in the car as a manager rather than on the coach as a player.

Kenny could be your friend as a player, but on a Thursday and Friday he would be ruthless as a manager. That was his job and it made him stand out as a manager better than anyone else. When he had to make a decision, he'd make it – whether it was right or wrong – and he was great for me.

Kenny looked after me the year that I decided to go to Juventus. I was getting hounded from the European press to do interviews and I just wanted to go and play football. Kenny pulled me to one side and asked 'what's wrong?' I explained all these people wanted to interview me and that I couldn't relax. He said 'leave it with me'. Kenny told the press that I wasn't doing any interviews on his say so. He took the blame from me onto his own shoulders. A lot of the press didn't like Kenny because I was now saying 'I'd love to do it, but the manager said I can't'.

Bob Paisley taught me everything, but as a man-manager, I've got a lot to thank Kenny for off the pitch. He knew if I wasn't right off the pitch, I wouldn't be right on it. He didn't just do that for me, he did it for everyone, for the sake of his players and the club.

'Kenny could be your friend as a player, but on a Thursday and Friday he would be ruthless as a manager'

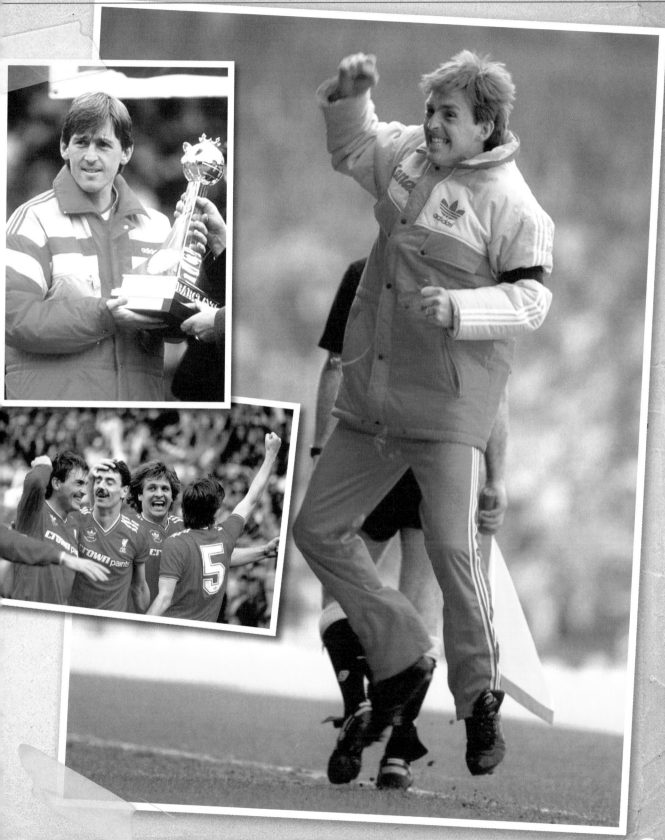

Graeme Souness Loved The Club

He was completely different to the other managers I'd played under. When Graeme took the job, I was made up. I knew him as a player and I knew he loved the club, but he just tried to change things too quickly.

He wanted the old players out and the new ones in, which was fair enough. But when it wasn't happening, he wanted the young players out and the old ones in, so he lost both sides of it. You can do that in Scotland, but not in England.

He had the right ideas, but you have to give people time to adapt. Graeme didn't and paid the price for that. Looking back now, I'm sure he realises he tried to change things too quickly.

We'd have two pre-seasons – Graeme's pre-season and Ronnie Moran's pre-season. Someone like Ronnie, who had been at the club for 40 years, had to try and adapt to things.

We had some great young players coming through, but you have to earn the right to be involved at Liverpool Football Club. It doesn't happen overnight. You have to work hard and you have to work as a team, not as individuals.

I think we started to have too many individuals and although we won the FA Cup, we never looked like winning the league. Individuals would be saying 'I played well'. It didn't matter because the team had lost.

Previous managers had a 'we're all in it together' attitude and I genuinely thought Graeme would have that too, but he tried to change things too quickly.

Roy Evans Did Well As LFC Manager

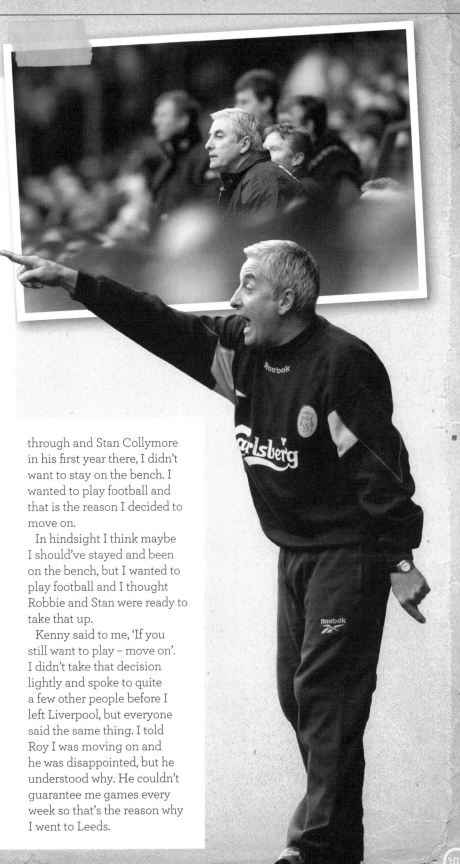

It was great playing under Roy and I was his captain from 1994 until 1996. I played under Roy in the Reserves and he joined the first team coaching side of things around the time I broke into the team, so he was like a mate to me.

Roy was most probably too nice – I don't know anyone who would not like him, he is the nicest person in the world. It was a big step for him, but he did well.

Look at his record as Liverpool manager: he finished third or fourth every year, but maybe the players got away with a bit more than they should have done.

One thing Souey had was that you wouldn't upset him. He'd be ruthless with you whereas Roy was completely the other way.

Doug Livermore came in to work with Roy and I knew Doug because I played with him at Chester and he was the assistant manager at Wales when Mike England was in charge. To me, it was like 'I've got two of my mates in charge here' and sometimes you can take things for granted in that situation. That's what happened.

Before I decided to leave Liverpool in 1996, I had a good chat with Kenny. With Robbie Fowler having come through and Stan Collymore in his first year there, I didn't want to stay on the bench. I wanted to play football and that is the reason I decided to move on.

In hindsight I think maybe I should've stayed and been on the bench, but I wanted to play football and I thought Robbie and Stan were ready to take that up.

Kenny said to me, 'If you still want to play – move on'. I didn't take that decision lightly and spoke to quite a few other people before I left Liverpool, but everyone said the same thing. I told Roy I was moving on and he was disappointed, but he understood why. He couldn't guarantee me games every week so that's the reason why I went to Leeds.

My Playing Partners

When it comes to double acts, I guess I'm most associated with Kenny Dalglish. Together we'd terrorise the opposition defence and have a great understanding of one another's game. He supplied many of my goals and it was a great partnership.

I also loved playing alongside John Aldridge. People say we couldn't play together, but when we did, one of us scored. We only played something like 20 times together, but I bet you we scored as many goals between us as we played games.

I also liked playing with Paul Walsh. Walshy was similar to Kenny, but a bit more of an individual player. You could liken him to Luis Suarez – Walshy was very tricky and he learned to play as a team player.

Peter Beardsley was another one. You didn't know what to expect from Peter; he had everything in his locker, but maybe being compared to Kenny was a bit too much for him.

On his day, if Peter wanted to find you, he would find you, he was that good. I didn't really get the time to gel with Nigel Clough, but he was another who everyone was looking at to be the new Kenny.

Paul, Peter, Nigel – they all looked like they could be a Kenny, but who was ever going to touch Kenny? No-one was ever going to get near him and I was spoiled to play alongside him.

In terms of adulation, the one who got nearest to Kenny was Robbie Fowler. The fans loved him.

When I was helping to bring Robbie along, I would tell him to do what Kenny used to tell me to do. When you first get in the team your job is to score goals and Robbie is a natural goalscorer.

He had terrible luck with injuries, but had he stayed fit, I think he could've come close to beating my goalscoring record.

I would do the running for him at first, but as things went on, he would do some running as well.

You have to make an instant impact when you are a young striker. Kenny gave that chance to me and I believe I gave that chance to Robbie. That's how you forge a partnership.

AWAY DAYS

I've travelled the planet as a footballer, visiting some incredible places and playing at some amazing stadiums. This is my passport to the world...

ITALY: THE REAL STORY

I think it was the morning after we'd completed the double by beating Everton at Wembley when serious speculation about me leaving Liverpool to go abroad really started.

Barcelona and Juventus were two of the clubs mentioned, but I didn't think too much of it until I spoke to Kenny and Peter Robinson. They admitted the stories were true – both clubs had made offers – and that Liverpool were prepared to sell me for financial reasons because the club was struggling, having been banned from Europe because of Heysel.

I was shocked. I loved it at Liverpool. My personal life was settled and I didn't want to leave, but I also thought that if the club are prepared to sell me, I'd have to consider going.

It was a difficult time. I was still living at my mum and dad's – me and Tracy were only due to get married the following summer – and to move away from home to a different country would be a big step for us.

Liverpool Echo, Tuesday April 21, 1987

HE'S ON HIS WAY TO ITALY

... AS A REAL HIGH-FLIER

IAN JOINS THE

JET SET

JUSTA ONE CORNETTO....

USEFUL ITALIAN PHRASES

LERN YERSELF ITALIAN

FRANK HARRIS

I spoke to both clubs and although Barcelona, managed by Terry Venables, made the better financial offer, I decided to sign for Juventus – after some sleepless nights – because I felt Serie A was the biggest stage to play on and that the Italian lifestyle would suit us better.

When I met with their president, Mr Boniperti, in London before making that decision, I did ask whether events at Heysel in 1985 would be held against me by the Juventus fans, but he assured me that wouldn't be the case. He was right. They were fantastic to me.

I travelled over to Turin with Peter Robinson for a supposedly secret meeting and something like 8,000 Juve fans turned up at the airport to meet me! It was unbelievable.

Because of the no-more-than-two-foreigners rule in place at the time, Juventus wanted to loan me out to Lazio for a season before calling me back to replace Michel Platini, who was planning to retire, for the start of 1987/88. I refused.

Lazio weren't even in Serie A, there was no way I was going there so I said why not let me stay for an extra season at Liverpool instead? That's exactly what happened.

It was one of those situations when I felt I needed to be honest to the Liverpool fans and admit that the transfer was for financial reasons, both for the club and myself, because I didn't want to end up in a position like Kevin Keegan did when he stayed at Anfield for a year after signing for Hamburg but annoyed some of the fans by saying he was leaving to 'further his career'.

So less than three weeks after getting married to Tracy and honeymooning in Aruba, we moved to Turin on July 20, 1987 and initially it was difficult because of the language barrier.

The difference in banter on the team coach and in the dressing room got me down, to be honest, and a conversation I had with Platini – who trained with us during pre-season to try and stay fit despite having retired – made me feel uneasy.

'Ian, I must tell you that you have picked the wrong time to come here. This is a bad team you are joining and I cannot see it getting any better.' He turned out to be a good judge!

I did well in pre-season, but a thigh injury that took longer to heal than first thought meant I started the season slowly, and by the time the Christmas break came, I had scored just five goals.

My Italian had improved a lot and I made friends with players like Sergio Brio, Stefano Tacconi and Pasquale Bruno, but the team was struggling and there wasn't a player who was making clear-cut chances for me like Kenny or Jan Molby did at Liverpool.

I spoke to Graeme Souness over Christmas about his time in Italy and his advice was for me to be more selfish. I listened to what he said and ended up scoring nine goals in the second half of the season, four in one cup game against Ascoli.

I settled more into the Italian way of life and little things made a difference to my fitness,

such as having a glass of water and a glass of wine with a post-match meal rather than beer, but we also missed our family and friends back home. I think we were racking up phone bills of more than £1,000-a-month!

I also returned to Anfield that May to play in Alan Hansen's testimonial and I remember the Liverpool fans giving me a fantastic reception and singing 'sign him on'. I thought to myself that if I ever came back to England to play, it would have to be for Liverpool.

That summer we went on holiday to the Cayman Islands and I developed what I thought were heat bumps. We flew back to the UK afterwards and I saw a doctor who told me I had chicken pox, shingles, hepatitis and a liver infection!

For three weeks I felt terrible. I was in pain, couldn't sleep and lost a lot of weight, which meant I felt exhausted when I started pre-season training with Juventus. Then I got a call from my adviser – 'Would you be interested in a return to Liverpool?'

To be honest, I jumped at the chance.

Juventus wanted to sell either me or Michael Laudrup because of the foreigners rule and Kenny wanted me back. It all happened very quickly after that.

Less than a week later, I was a Liverpool player again and I was made up to be back. We bought a lovely house on the Wirral and still live there now.

I know people say it didn't work out for me in Italy, but moving there for a year was one of the best things I've ever done. I'd most probably have stayed there for the rest of my career had I not returned to Liverpool that summer.

Italy was a great life experience for us and it also led to perhaps the most famous quote ever attributed to me – 'Playing in Italy was like playing in a foreign country.'

The funny thing is that it wasn't me who said those words. It was Kenny Dalglish!

When I was moving back to Liverpool, the club had managed to keep the story out of the papers, but after the press conference to announce my return, a reporter cornered Kenny hoping for a

quote that no-one else had got. He asked if I'd said anything in private about my time in Italy, so Kenny, being Kenny, decided to wind him up and replied 'he said playing in Italy was like playing in a foreign country!'

Next thing, it's in the paper and taken as gospel that I said it. Over 25 years on and people still remind me of that quote now.

I suppose I owe Kenny one for that – but then I also owe him for bringing me back to Liverpool.

Who knows how things would've turned out for me if he hadn't?

A True Red
On The Beach

I was badly burnt when I was 18 or 19 and had just signed for Liverpool. I went to Benidorm with the lads from Flint and I don't think any of us had been to Spain before. We got there and fell asleep on the beach and got burnt. For the rest of the holiday, we all struggled. That was the first proper taste of the sun I'd had – we were there for a week – and I really burnt myself.

When we were playing, no-one wore suncream, but I'm very lucky because I catch the sun pretty easily and go brown. Saying that, there was a time when I was playing for Wales in Malta and before the game we could smell coconut oil in the dressing room. Clayton Blackmore, who played for Man United and used to go on the sunbeds, had rubbed coconut suntan oil in because we were in Malta. I think he thought he was on his holidays.

I like sitting by the pool, but the only problem is I get bored after an hour. I wouldn't say I'm a great reader, I prefer to watch films or listen to music. Once I feel my batteries have been recharged, I get bored and I can't keep still so I end up going for walks instead.

Malaysia

DUBAI

Clayton Blackmore

Home From Home

I love going to Portugal. I've got a holiday home there and I've been going there for over 25 years for breaks. Malaysia and the islands in that area are beautiful and one place I'd love to go back to is Mauritius. I've been there once and I love tropical islands like that, but getting the right time of year to go is difficult for me. I was actually in Malaysia for four weeks during the last World Cup and my family came over to stay for a week. There would be monkeys coming down from the trees after our food – I've never experienced anything like it before. Places like Dubai are also incredible to go to.

Happy days. Relaxing on holiday with my family

Culture Club

I've enjoyed experiencing the different cultures in my role as Liverpool FC ambassador, which I'll talk about in more detail later. China is amazing. I never really thought I would go there, let alone experience the culture of the Chinese people in the way I have. To walk on the Great Wall of China and visit the Forbidden City were incredible experiences. The Far East – Thailand, Malaysia – is incredible and the thing I did learn from going there is that you never stop learning about different countries.

The Liverpool fans in the Far East are incredible. Until you go over there, you don't realise how fanatical they are. They would give anything to go to Anfield, but because there are so many Liverpool supporters there, I think we have to take the club to them. »

115

When I was a kid, people would say it is a big wide world out there, but the world is becoming smaller and smaller now. It is easy to travel to other parts of the world and it is great to see how fanatical the Liverpool supporters are.

Even the likes of myself, when I travel as an ambassador, get a fantastic reaction because I'm representing Liverpool Football Club, so imagine what it is like when the first team go there. They're like Gods out there and that is down to the brand of Liverpool Football Club.

I spoke to the players after the tour of Asia last year and the new players couldn't believe there were 40,000 there to watch them train. I went to open a shop and there were 5,000 people there waiting to see me, wanting my autograph. It just shows how fanatical the supporters are in Asia.

Getting Spotted By The Fans

I get plenty of banter at Manchester, but lots at Liverpool too because there are Reds and Blues there. In fairness, the banter at Manchester Airport is good natured, but I have to say I get recognised more when I'm abroad than at the airports here. It always seems like more people spot me in London, too.

In Liverpool, when someone recognises me, they'll just shout my name and 'hello' and then carry on about their business. But when I'm in London, or anywhere abroad, they'll want autographs and all that. It means it sometimes takes me longer to get where I'm going, but I don't mind that.

When I came back from Juventus, Ronnie was rooming with Steve McMahon so Jan Molby became my room-mate. I had some great times, especially rooming with Jan

My Room-mates

Before I went to Juventus, Ronnie Whelan was my room-mate. Ronnie was the best man at my wedding and we get on really well. We broke into the first team at exactly the same time, having been in the Reserves. Ronnie and Kevin Sheedy looked after me in the Reserves at Liverpool and I've got a lot to thank them for.

Everyone expected Kevin to take Ray Kennedy's place, but for some reason Bob Paisley put Ronnie in on the left-hand side when he had been playing in the middle.

Ronnie made that position his own and I happened to break into the first team at the same time, so Ronnie Moran put us together. When I came back from Juventus, Ronnie was rooming with Steve McMahon so Jan Molby became my room-mate. I had some great times, especially rooming with Jan.

Trouble On The Road

As a player, you're in and out of most places, especially when you're at Liverpool. We used to get to a place as late as possible and leave straight after games. When you're in places like Russia, things are very different and we had some tough trips there, especially with Wales. I remember having to go via Moscow to get to Tbilisi – I think it took us 24 hours.

As an ambassador, the only problem I've had was in Egypt. I loved the country, but I was involved in a car crash. The roads are not the best in Egypt and the drivers are even worse! A car knocked into the side of us and we hit a wall. Fortunately, the wall collapsed on impact. If the wall hadn't collapsed, it would most probably have been far more dangerous for those of us who were in the car. The wall collapsing saved us.

We were in the middle of Cairo and even though we had crashed, other cars were still beeping us and going past at 60 or 70mph. It wasn't the best of experiences, but then we also visited the Pyramids in Egypt and that was fantastic. We were on our way there when we crashed, so it was going from one extreme to the other. I never thought I'd see the Pyramids, so to experience one of the great wonders of the world, on a camel, was great.

A Good Laugh Always On The Cards

We used to play cards on the bus or plane – me, Ronnie, Alan Hansen and Steve Nicol. Steve Nicol was the worst! We used to play 'Hearts' and Hansen would always sit next to Nicol. If I was leading, I'd always put Nicol in to play the next card and he'd inevitably play it so Hansen ended up taking a hit.

I couldn't say some of the things that Hansen called Nicol at the time, but it was really funny for the rest of us. Hansen was probably the biggest shark. He was the best card player, but he often lost because we'd set Nicol up to ensure he took the hit.

We had a good laugh doing that and the team spirit played a big part in how we did on the pitch.

It was brilliant and that's what it is all about if you're going to be successful – team spirit, both on and off the pitch. They used to call me, Jan, Ronnie and Steve McMahon 'the gang' because we had a great laugh together.

Bruce Grobbelaar and Steve Nicol were big characters in the dressing room and everyone used to take the mickey out of Nico. He was the butt of the jokes, but he took it all well. Bruce was just Bruce. It didn't matter if you were playing well or playing badly, Bruce would always cheer you up and was great to have in the dressing room.

My Favourite European Away Trip

I know it's easy for me to say this, but my favourite has to be the 1984 European Cup final in Rome. We played in Bucharest in the semi-final – we won 2-1 and I scored two goals there – and afterwards we were all excited. Joe Fagan made us all quieten down in the dressing room and started saying "I don't know what you're all getting carried away for." There was complete silence and suddenly Joe jumped into the air and shouted "yippee!"

"Now you can celebrate," he said. "I just wanted to do it first!" Joe was so excited that we'd got to the final and to actually play Roma in Rome, and beat them there, was incredible.

To tell you the truth, we went there feeling like we were invincible. We were so confident that we were going to win. In the tunnel we were all singing the Chris Rea song 'I Don't Know What It Is But I Love It' and the Italians thought there was something wrong with us.

When I ended up moving to Italy I remember some of them asking me 'what were you doing? Why were you singing?' It was all about team spirit and we took that onto the pitch in Rome. To beat them at their own place and lift the European Cup – it's a night I'll never forget.

Rome '84 – what a night! I don't know if we're singing a Chris Rea song here...

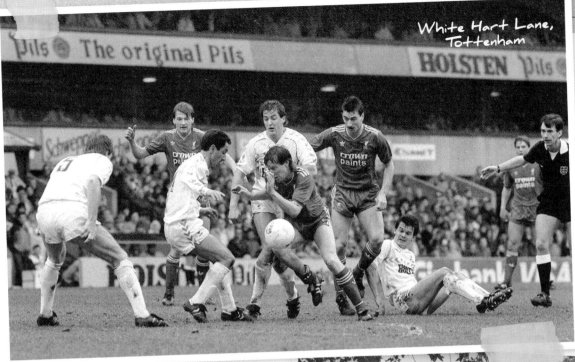
White Hart Lane, Tottenham

My Best And Worst Away Grounds

I never liked playing at Old Trafford because I hardly ever scored there, but I liked playing at Goodison Park because I supported them as a kid and always did well there. Everton was my favourite, but I loved playing at Tottenham as well. White Hart Lane is a nice ground. I enjoyed going to Manchester City, too, and you only enjoy certain grounds if you do well there.

San Siro in Milan

There was always a great atmosphere at Man United, but I only scored one goal at Old Trafford.

One of the most difficult grounds to go to was The Den, Millwall's old ground. They were right on top of you and it was a frightening experience.

At Juventus, I loved playing at the San Siro against Inter and AC Milan – that was probably the best experience of them all – and also at Napoli. Even though their ground was further back from the pitch, there were 80,000 in there.

The fans can make a lot of noise, but you just have to blank it out. Even when we played Fiorentina in Florence – there's a big historical

The (old) Den, Millwall

»

rivalry between them and Juventus – the abuse we got was unbelievable. A lot of it was aimed at me, but you have to learn to blank it out.

It's the same when people are singing your name. If you don't blank it out, you can get too carried away and that is one of the secrets of being successful on the pitch. I could be playing in front of one person or 100,000 people, but as soon as the game starts, I'd blank out everything else. I could hear the Liverpool fans singing my name when I'd scored, but I would still concentrate on what was happening on the pitch. That's what makes you a proper professional. I always remember Bob Paisley saying 'if you read the papers when you're playing well, read them when you're playing badly'. It's the same when the supporters are singing about you.

For a lot of teams coming to Anfield, they were already beaten because they couldn't ignore the noise that was happening around them. You could easily wind players up as well and if they spoke back to you then you knew it was working. People used to try that with me but as soon as they started talking to me I saw it as the first sign of them not concentrating, so I didn't react. If I was talking back I'd have been losing my concentration as well, and when you're a striker, it is a split second that makes the difference between scoring a goal and not.

Pride And Pain Of Playing For Wales

I loved playing at Wrexham, because it was a smaller crowd, but when we went to the Cardiff Arms Park, there would be 70,000 there. It was incredible. I played at a time when we went unbeaten for a number of years at Cardiff Arms Park and we felt invincible. Beating World Champions Germany there stands out, but then so does the night when we had to beat Romania to qualify for the 1994 World Cup. We lost 2-1, the first time we'd been beaten at the Arms Park in years and that devastated us.

Wales 1
Germany 0

Wembley Dream Comes True

As a kid, I dreamed of scoring the winning goal at Wembley. Wembley is my favourite stadium of all time, simply because my boyhood dream came true there. The first time I played there for Wales, in the Home Internationals, I scored, but we got beat 2-1. It was still a great experience though. Playing there for Liverpool was unbelievable and it will always be my favourite ground.

I always say to kids that you have to have a dream. They may not come true, but you have to try and live your dream. When I scored the winning goals for Liverpool at Wembley in the FA Cup final, my dream came true.

Winning the double against Everton at Wembley in 1986 and winning the FA Cup at Wembley after the Hillsborough disaster in 1989 were different experiences. '86 was the best from an individual point of view. It was the year we did the double, we

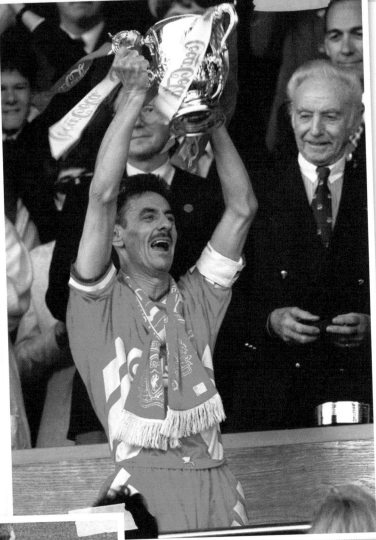

I enjoyed lifting the League Cup at Wembley in 1995, too

beat Everton and to be 1-0 down at half-time only to go on and win 3-1 in my first FA Cup final was special. It was the first time Liverpool had ever won the double so it was everything rolled into one and that was a night when I didn't go to bed! There are a few stories about me coming back on the bus the next day and I think you can tell I'd been up all night!

Wembley Woe

I ended up on the losing side at Wembley to Arsenal in the League Cup in '87 and Man United in the FA Cup in '96, which were ironically the last seasons of my two spells at Liverpool.

I counted the '87 strike in my memorable goals section earlier, but ultimately I felt really bad because it was the first time I had scored and we lost. We played in white that day and I scored first when Steve McMahon set me up for a nice side-foot into the corner. To then lose at Wembley, and for it

to be my first experience of losing, having scored for Liverpool, was awful. If you look at the two goals Arsenal scored, they were own goals. Charlie Nicholas claimed them, but they were scrappy goals.

Every time I had scored for Liverpool in almost seven years, we had never lost. I remember Gary Lineker saying in an interview after we beat Everton in '86 that my equaliser won that final because all the players on the pitch knew that Liverpool never lose when I score. The opposition were thinking they wouldn't win because I had equalised and that's what happened. In '87, I found it hard to take in that we had lost after I'd scored, but all great things come to an end. The following week we played Norwich and we got beaten again after I had scored!

The worst feeling of all, though, was in '96 because I knew that was my last game for Liverpool.

RETURN OF THE GOAL RUSH

When I came back from Italy, the goals kept coming. Here are some strikes from my second spell at Anfield that stand out in the memory...

20.05.89

v Everton, Wembley, FA Cup Final

I started this game on the bench but
Everton couldn't keep me quiet when I
did come on! Steve Nicol drifted a great
ball into the box, I held off my Wales
team-mate Kevin Ratcliffe, swivelled and
hammered home.

20.05.89

v Everton, Wembley, FA Cup Final

The winning goal in this match was all
down to a great John Barnes cross from
the left. At 2-2 in extra-time the game was
anybody's, but John produced the perfect
delivery and I managed to head past
Neville Southall to win it.

23.05.89

**v West Ham United, Anfield,
Football League Division One**

This was our second to last game of
the season and we needed to win to
stay on course for the title. We did it in
style, beating West Ham 5-1. I scored
in the 84th minute after Ray Houghton
(2) and John Aldridge had found the
net. Barnesie got the last goal

'I picked the ball up
outside the box, sold
Julian Dicks a huge
dummy before slamming
home at the Kop end'

09.09.89

v Derby County, Baseball Ground, Football League Division One

It might not be the prettiest but they all count. This was a classic 'me' goal. One yard out. I dived in and got the last touch – it's the scoreboard that matters most!

Chelsea double: Both goals at Stamford Bridge in 1989 were enjoyable while the goal against Derby (top) was a close-range special!

16.12.89

v Chelsea, Stamford Bridge, Football League Division One

It was always nice to beat Chelsea at their ground and this 5-2 victory was one of the best. I chipped Dave Beasant to get the ball rolling.

16.12.89

Chelsea, Stamford Bridge, Football League Division One

I couldn't head the ball apparently... but this goal would suggest otherwise! A back post bullet effort left Beasant with no chance.

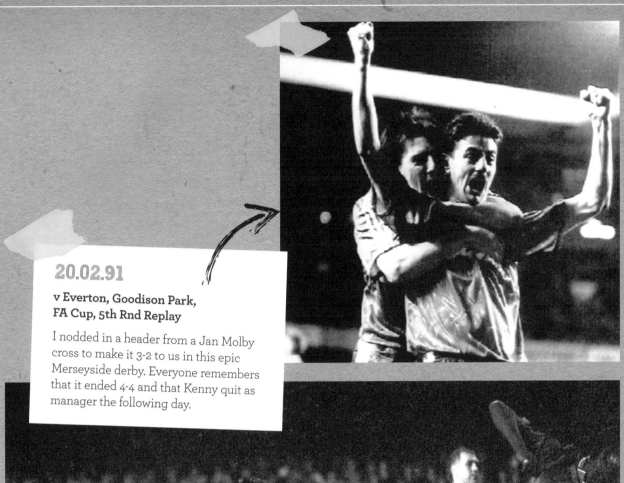

20.02.91

**v Everton, Goodison Park,
FA Cup, 5th Rnd Replay**

I nodded in a header from a Jan Molby
cross to make it 3-2 to us in this epic
Merseyside derby. Everyone remembers
that it ended 4-4 and that Kenny quit as
manager the following day.

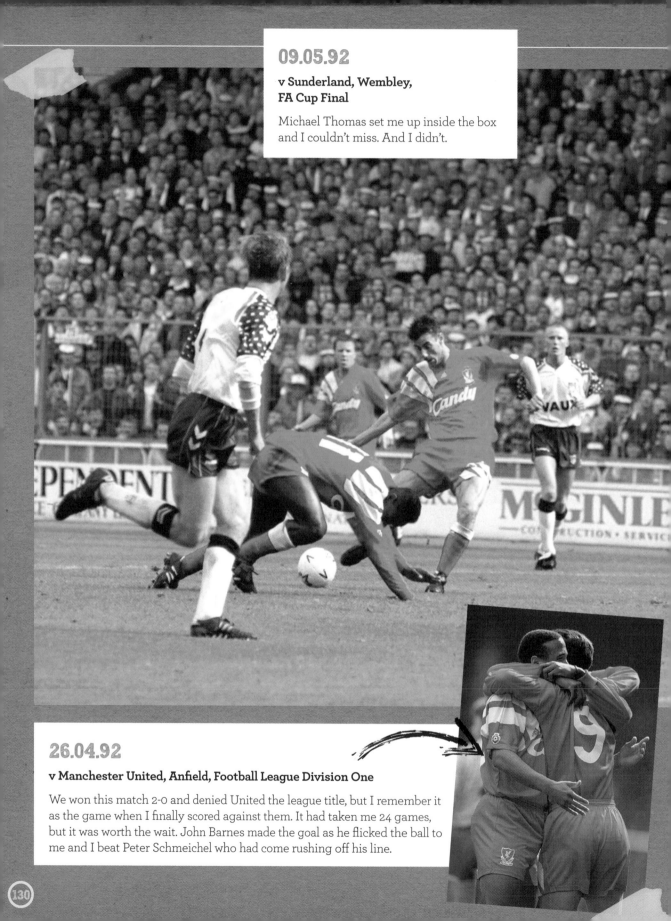

09.05.92

**v Sunderland, Wembley,
FA Cup Final**

Michael Thomas set me up inside the box
and I couldn't miss. And I didn't.

26.04.92

v Manchester United, Anfield, Football League Division One

We won this match 2-0 and denied United the league title, but I remember it
as the game when I finally scored against them. It had taken me 24 games,
but it was worth the wait. John Barnes made the goal as he flicked the ball to
me and I beat Peter Schmeichel who had come rushing off his line.

'Scoring at Wembley never gets boring!'

18.10.92

v Manchester United, Old Trafford, Premier League

This was my first goal at Old Trafford – and it took me past Roger Hunt as Liverpool's all-time highest goalscorer. That remains a massive honour and although United scored late on to earn a 2-2 draw, it was still a proud moment. My goal came just before half-time when Ronny Rosenthal found me unmarked seven yards out and I did the rest.

28.12.92

v Manchester City, Anfield, Premier League

Steve McManaman did brilliantly on the wing then crossed perfectly which allowed me to steady myself and fire home one of the best volleys I ever scored.

08.05.93

v Tottenham Hotspur, Anfield, Premier League

We ended the season in style as we thrashed Spurs 6-2 at home and I managed to score my 300th goal for the club. John Barnes passed from the left and I thrashed a right-footed effort past Ian Walker.

27.10.93

v Ipswich Town, Anfield, League Cup, 3rd Rnd

I'd scored my first two goals within the opening 15 minutes but I had to wait until after the break for my third, sliding in at the back post to get the last touch to a Robbie Fowler pass.

13.03.94

v Everton, Anfield, Premier League

This was the last derby the Kop enjoyed as a terraced stand so it was nice to send the place crazy one last time. We held on against a determined Everton side to win 2-1 and I managed to score our first as I latched on to Julian Dicks' through-ball before volleying past Neville Southall. It was also my last derby goal.

30.11.94

v Blackburn Rovers, Ewood Park, League Cup, 4th Rnd

I scored a hat-trick in this game and my opening goal was the best. I fired a left-foot shot from outside the box that left Blackburn goalkeeper Tim Flowers with no chance.

26.12.94

v Leicester City, Filbert Street, Premier League

A nice late Christmas present! Some brilliant and patient build-up play from John Barnes and Steve McManaman finally released Robbie Fowler down the left and I got the last touch to his great cross. A real team effort that I was thrilled to finish off.

11.01.95

v Arsenal, Anfield, League Cup, 5th Rnd

John Barnes and Neil Ruddock set this goal up with a wonderful free-kick move. All I had to do was finish it off inside the box – something I was more than happy to do! This goal came on the path to winning the only trophy while I was captain, so I have fond memories of that League Cup campaign.

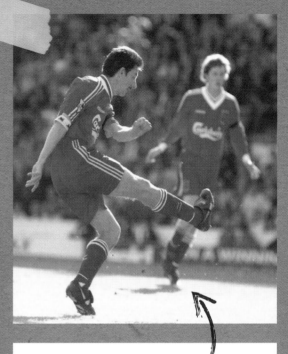

05.05.96

Manchester City, Maine Road, Premier League

My last Liverpool goal has to be included doesn't it? We broke forward through Robbie Fowler and Steve McManaman and I tried my luck from 25 yards – and it flew past Eike Immel into the back of the net.

28.02.95

v Wimbledon, Selhurst Park, FA Cup, 5th Rnd Replay

The goal saw me equal Denis Law's FA Cup scoring record as I hit my 41st Cup strike. Steve McManaman and John Barnes linked up and I slid home to sit alongside the Manchester United great.

06.01.96

Rochdale, Anfield, FA Cup, 3rd Rnd

I became the leading all-time FA Cup scorer in this game – but Stan Collymore tried to steal my limelight with a hat-trick! I had Robbie Fowler to thank for this goal as he released me in the box and I slotted past Rochdale keeper Chris Clarke.

Goals By Season (1988-1996)

1988/89

Date	Opposition	H/A	Competition	Result
208) 12/10/88	Walsall	A	League Cup	3-1
209) 26/10/88	Nottingham Forest	A	Division One	1-2
210) 29/10/88	West Ham	A	Division One	2-0
211) 05/11/88	Middlesbrough	H	Division One	3-0
212) 26/12/88	Derby County	A	Division One	1-0
213) 21/01/89	Southampton	H	Division One	2-0
214) 29/01/89	Millwall	A	FA Cup	2-0
215) 04/02/89	Newcastle United	A	Division One	2-2
216) 20/05/89	Everton	N	FA Cup	3-2
217) 20/05/89	Everton	N	FA Cup	3-2
218) 23/05/89	West Ham United	H	Division One	5-1

1989/90

Date	Opposition	H/A	Competition	Result
219) 09/09/89	Derby County	A	Division One	3-0
220) 12/09/89	Crystal Palace	H	Division One	9-0
221) 19/09/89	Wigan Athletic	H	League Cup	5-2
222) 19/09/89	Wigan Athletic	H	League Cup	5-2
223) 23/03/89	Everton	A	Division One	3-1
224) 23/03/89	Everton	A	Division One	3-1
225) 19/11/89	Millwall	A	Division One	2-1
226) 02/12/89	Manchester City	A	Division One	4-1
227) 02/12/89	Manchester City	A	Division One	4-1
228) 16/12/89	Chelsea	A	Division One	5-2
229) 16/12/89	Chelsea	A	Division One	5-2
230) 26/12/89	Sheffield Wednesday	H	Division One	2-1
231) 01/01/90	Nottingham Forest	A	Division One	2-2
232) 01/01/90	Nottingham Forest	A	Division One	2-2
233) 09/01/90	Swansea City	H	FA Cup	8-0
234) 09/01/90	Swansea City	H	FA Cup	8-0
235) 09/01/90	Swansea City	H	FA Cup	8-0
236) 20/01/90	Crystal Palace	A	Division One	2-0
237) 17/02/90	Southampton	H	FA Cup	3-0
238) 11/03/90	QPR	A	FA Cup	2-2
239) 31/03/90	Southampton	H	Division One	3-2
240) 03/04/90	Wimbledon	H	Division One	2-1
241) 08/04/90	Crystal Palace	N	FA Cup	3-4
242) 21/04/90	Chelsea	H	Division One	4-1
243) 28/04/90	QPR	H	Division One	2-1
244) 05/05/90	Coventry City	A	Division One	6-1

1990/91

Date	Opposition	H/A	Competition	Result
245) 25/08/90	Sheffield United	A	Division One	3-1
246) 28/08/90	Nottingham Forest	H	Division One	2-0
247) 25/09/90	Crewe Alexandra	H	League Cup	5-1
248) 25/09/90	Crewe Alexandra	H	League Cup	5-1
249) 09/10/90	Crewe Alexandra	A	League Cup	4-1
250) 09/10/90	Crewe Alexandra	A	League Cup	4-1
251) 09/10/90	Crewe Alexandra	A	League Cup	4-1
252) 27/10/90	Chelsea	H	Division One	2-0
253) 04/11/90	Tottenham Hotspur	A	Division One	3-1
254) 04/11/90	Tottenham Hotspur	A	Division One	3-1
255) 10/11/90	Luton Town	H	Division One	4-0
256) 10/11/90	Luton Town	H	Division One	4-0
257) 24/11/90	Manchester City	H	Division One	2-2
258) 15/12/90	Sheffield United	H	Division One	2-0
259) 01/01/91	Leeds United	H	Division One	3-0
260) 08/01/91	Blackburn Rovers	H	FA Cup	3-0
261) 26/01/91	Brighton	H	FA Cup	2-2
262) 26/01/91	Brighton	H	FA Cup	2-2
263) 30/01/91	Brighton	H	FA Cup	3-2
264) 20/02/91	Everton	A	FA Cup	4-4

Date	Opposition	H/A	Competition	Result
265) 16/03/91	Sunderland	H	Division One	2-1
266) 23/03/91	Derby County	H	Division One	7-1
267) 09/04/91	Coventry City	H	Division One	1-1
268) 20/04/91	Norwich City	H	Division One	3-0
269) 23/04/91	Crystal Palace	H	Division One	3-0
270) 11/05/91	Tottenham Hotspur	H	Division One	2-0

1991/92

Date	Opposition	H/A	Competition	Result
271) 25/09/91	Stoke City	H	League Cup	2-2
272) 25/09/91	Stoke City	H	League Cup	2-2
273) 19/10/91	Chelsea	A	Division One	2-2
274) 29/10/91	Port Vale	H	League Cup	2-2
275) 18/03/92	Genoa	H	UEFA Cup	1-2
276) 31/03/92	Notts County	H	Division One	4-0
277) 22/04/92	Nottingham Forest	A	Division One	2-2
278) 26/04/92	Manchester United	H	Division One	2-0
279) 09/05/91	Sunderland	N	FA Cup	2-0

1992/93

Date	Opposition	H/A	Competition	Result
280) 08/08/92	Leeds United	N	Charity Shield	3-4
281) 16/09/92	Apollon Limassol	H	European CWC	6-1
282) 16/09/92	Apollon Limassol	H	European CWC	6-1
283) 16/09/92	Apollon Limassol	H	European CWC	6-1
284) 16/09/92	Apollon Limassol	H	European CWC	6-1
285) 16/09/92	Apollon Limassol	H	European CWC	6-1
286) 06/10/92	Chesterfield	A	League Cup	4-1
287) 18/10/92	Manchester United	A	Premier League	2-2
288) 07/11/92	Middlesbrough	H	Premier League	4-1
289) 28/12/92	Manchester City	H	Premier League	1-1
290) 03/01/93	Bolton Wanderers	A	FA Cup	2-2
291) 06/03/93	Manchester United	H	Premier League	1-2
292) 10/03/93	QPR	H	Premier League	1-0
293) 13/03/93	Middlesbrough	A	Premier League	2-1
294) 23/03/93	Crystal Palace	A	Premier League	1-1
295) 03/04/93	Blackburn Rovers	A	Premier League	1-4
296) 10/04/93	Oldham Athletic	H	Premier League	1-0
297) 12/04/93	Manchester City	A	Premier League	1-1
298) 05/05/93	Oldham Athletic	A	Premier League	2-3
299) 05/05/93	Oldham Athletic	A	Premier League	2-3
300) 08/05/93	Tottenham Hotspur	H	Premier League	6-2
301) 08/05/93	Tottenham Hotspur	H	Premier League	6-2

1993/94

Date	Opposition	H/A	Competition	Result
302) 18/08/93	QPR	A	Premier League	3-1
303) 28/08/93	Leeds United	H	Premier League	2-0

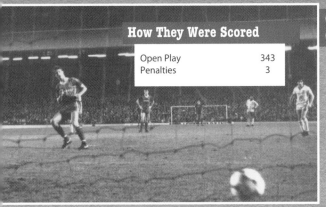

How They Were Scored

Open Play	343
Penalties	3

Goals By Opposition

Opponents	Total
Everton	25
Manchester City	15
Coventry City	15
Southampton	13
Ipswich Town	13
Tottenham Hotspur	13
QPR	11
Aston Villa	10
Chelsea	10
Nottingham Forest	10
Watford	10
Leicester City	9
Luton Town	9
Newcastle United	9
Norwich City	9
Birmingham City	8
Notts County	8
Sheffield Wednesday	8
Swansea City	8
West Ham United	8
Arsenal	7
Crystal Palace	7
Blackburn Rovers	6
Leeds United	6
Oxford United	6
Stoke City	6
Sunderland	6
Apollon Limassol	5
Benfica	5
Brighton & Hove Albion	5
Crewe Alexandra	5
Oldham Athletic	5
Exeter City	4
Fulham	4
Middlesbrough	4
Wimbledon	4
Barnsley	3
Derby County	3
Manchester United	3
Sheffield United	3
Brentford	2
Dinamo Bucharest	2
Millwall	2
Panathinaikos	2
Walsall	2
West Bromwich Albion	2
Wigan Athletic	2
AZ Alkmaar	1
Athletic Bilbao	1
Bolton Wanderers	1
Bristol City	1
Charlton Athletic	1
Chesterfield	1
Dundalk	1
Genoa	1
Oulu Palloseura	1
Port Vale	1
Rochdale	1
Widzew Lodz	1
Wolverhampton Wanderers	1
York City	1

Goals By Competition

Competition	Total
Division One	184
Premier League	45
FA Cup	39
League Cup	48
European Cup	14
UEFA Cup	1
European Cup Winners' Cup	5
Charity Shield	3
Screen Sport Super Cup	7

Goals When Started/Substitute

Started	340
Substitute	6

• Liverpool score shown first

	Date	Opposition	H/A	Competition	Result
304)	22/09/93	Fulham	A	League Cup	3-1
305)	23/10/93	Man City	A	Premier League	1-1
306)	27/10/93	Ipswich Town	H	League Cup	3-2
307)	27/10/93	Ipswich Town	H	League Cup	3-2
308)	27/10/93	Ipswich Town	H	League Cup	3-2
309)	30/10/93	Southampton	H	Premier League	4-2
310)	08/12/93	QPR	H	Premier League	3-2
311)	01/01/94	Ipswich Town	A	Premier League	2-1
312)	19/01/94	Bristol City	A	FA Cup	1-1
313)	22/01/94	Man City	H	Premier League	2-1
314)	22/01/94	Man City	H	Premier League	2-1
315)	14/02/94	Southampton	A	Premier League	2-4
316)	26/02/94	Coventry City	H	Premier League	1-0
317)	13/03/94	Everton	H	Premier League	2-1
318)	19/03/94	Chelsea	H	Premier League	2-1
319)	02/04/94	Sheffield United	H	Premier League	1-2
320)	23/04/94	West Ham	A	Premier League	2-1

1994/95

	Date	Opposition	H/A	Competition	Result
321)	20/08/94	Crystal Palace	A	Premier League	6-1
322)	20/08/94	Crystal Palace	A	Premier League	6-1
323)	24/09/94	Newcastle United	A	Premier League	1-1
324)	01/10/94	Sheffield Wednesday	H	Premier League	4-1
325)	25/10/94	Stoke City	H	League Cup	2-1
326)	25/10/94	Stoke City	H	League Cup	2-1
327)	30/11/94	Blackburn Rovers	A	League Cup	3-1
328)	30/11/94	Blackburn Rovers	A	League Cup	3-1
329)	30/11/94	Blackburn Rovers	A	League Cup	3-1
330)	03/12/94	Coventry City	A	Premier League	1-1
331)	26/12/94	Leicester City	A	Premier League	2-1
332)	02/01/95	Norwich City	H	Premier League	4-0
333)	11/01/95	Arsenal	H	League Cup	1-0
334)	28/02/95	Wimbledon	A	FA Cup	2-0
335)	04/03/95	Newcastle United	H	Premier League	2-0
336)	05/04/95	Southampton	H	Premier League	3-1
337)	05/04/95	Southampton	H	Premier League	3-1
338)	17/04/95	Leicester City	H	Premier League	2-0
339)	29/04/95	Norwich City	A	Premier League	2-1

1995/96

	Date	Opposition	H/A	Competition	Result
340)	25/10/95	Manchester City	H	League Cup	4-0
341)	28/10/95	Manchester City	H	Premier League	6-0
342)	28/10/95	Manchester City	H	Premier League	6-0
343)	04/11/95	Newcastle United	A	Premier League	1-2
344)	06/01/96	Rochdale	H	FA Cup	7-0
345)	13/01/96	Sheffield Wednesday	A	Premier League	1-1
346)	05/05/96	Manchester City	A	Premier League	2-2

SHIRT SWAPS

10 · 9

BAYERN MÜNCHEN

10

I've got three shirts framed on my walls at home, one of them is my own shirt from the 1986 FA Cup Final win over Everton. The other two were shirts from European legends who asked me if I would swap with them. It's been fun getting my big box down from the loft to look at some of the other shirts I've kept. Take a look and I'll talk you through the ones I've picked out...

The Magic
NUMBER

I'd Have Worn Any Number For Liverpool

I was just given the number 9 at Liverpool by Bob Paisley. I never asked for anything. If they'd given me number 2 at Liverpool, I'd have taken it. David Johnson wore number 9 and I was taking his place in the team so I automatically got that shirt. For me, it was the best thing that happened because people always say number 7 and 9 are the two best shirts at Liverpool. Keegan and Dalglish had 7 and Robbie took number 9 off me when I left. If you've worn those two shirts, you've done well.

I Used To Prefer The Number 10

I always loved wearing number 10 when I was at Chester! I wore 9 for Deeside Primary Schools, but for some reason I always wore number 10 when I was in the Reserves at Chester. It was only when I got in the first team, when Ian Edwards went to Wrexham, that they gave me the number 9 shirt. Had they asked me, I'd have said I'll have number 10, but I got the 9, started scoring and became synonymous with the number.

1978-1979 Chester Away
One Of My First Professional Shirts

I only played 34 games for Chester between 1978 and 1980 but I still have loads of affection for them. This was my away shirt from my first season. I think the yellow kit changed slightly for the next season when we shocked Newcastle in the third round of the FA Cup. I scored in that game and we went all the way to the last 16 with Ipswich eventually putting us out. My last game for Chester was unbelievable. The fans knew I was leaving. On the final whistle they invaded the pitch and mobbed me. All I could hear was 'All the best for the future' and 'Thanks for everything you've done'.

1982-1985 Liverpool Home
An Old Favourite

We'd been playing in the old Hitachi kits for a couple of seasons when this pinstripe home shirt was introduced. The pinstripe came in the year before but only on the yellow away shirt. On this one, the stripes were only on the front. Some fans won't realise that we weren't allowed to have Crown Paints on the front when we were playing televised games during the 1982-83 season. It's not my actual shirt from the 1984 European Cup Final in Rome, but it reminds me of doing the treble and we won two titles, including our third in a row, wearing it.

1985 European Cup Final
We'll Never Forget The Heysel Disaster

The game is irrelevant and it's not a shirt that you keep for pride reasons, but it's amazing that I went on to play for Juventus after what happened.

My FAVOURITE SHIRT

1986 FA Cup Final
Taking Pride Of Place

This is the shirt that I have framed above the fireplace in my snooker room. I obviously had the fortune of scoring twice against Everton at Wembley on two occasions to win the FA Cup, which is the stuff of dreams. But nothing beats doing it for the first time. I'm really proud of this one.

ITALIAN Fashion

1987 Juventus Home
Scoring On My Home Deb

This is the shirt I wore for my home debu
for Juventus on September 27th, 1987.
scored twice in a 3-1 win over Pescara. I
was an incredible feeling playing in fron
of the Juve fans in the Stadio Comunale
People look back and tend to think I
wasn't successful during my season in
Italy, but I actually finished top scorer fo
Juventus.

1987 Juventus Away
A Nice Pink Number

The fabric on this jersey is like a
thick woollen jumper your nan
would knit. The colour is one
thing, and it goes back to when
Juventus were first formed and
playing in a pink and black kit,
but wearing this in the heat was
uncomfortable at times. Having
said that, it's such an unusual
shirt that it stands out in my
collection.

'89 CUP FINAL

1989 FA Cup Final Shirt
I Wasn't Wearing My Number 9 That Day

This shirt has special significance to me, being a 1989 FA Cup Final Shirt...

It's special in two ways. Not just because we beat Everton in an all-Merseyside Cup Final.

On the reverse of the shirt, there's an unfamiliar number 14 on it. That's when I came on as a sub and I refused to wear number 12. I just felt 12 was unlucky so every time I was sub, I was always number 14.

»

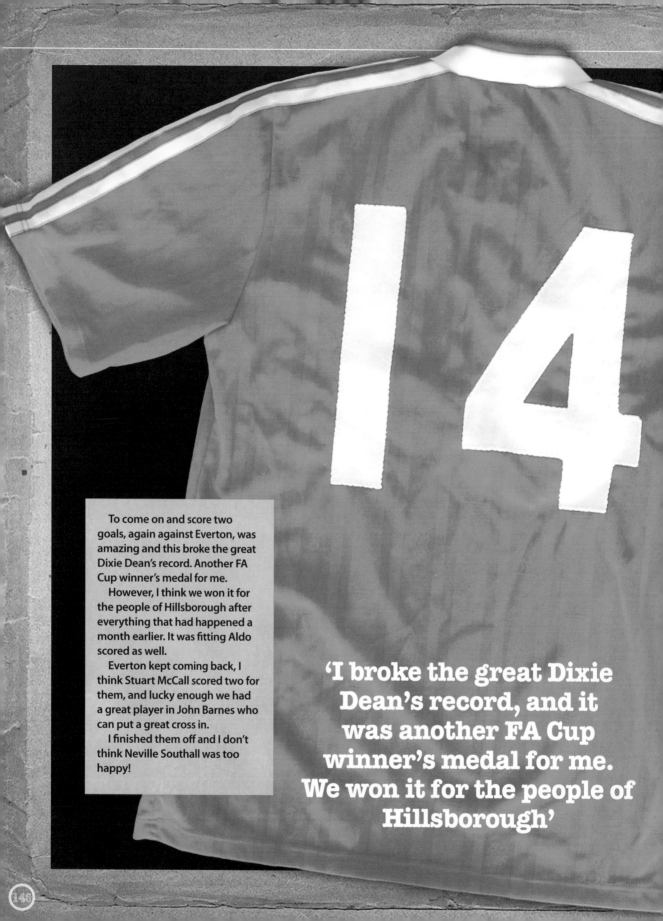

To come on and score two goals, again against Everton, was amazing and this broke the great Dixie Dean's record. Another FA Cup winner's medal for me.

However, I think we won it for the people of Hillsborough after everything that had happened a month earlier. It was fitting Aldo scored as well.

Everton kept coming back, I think Stuart McCall scored two for them, and lucky enough we had a great player in John Barnes who can put a great cross in.

I finished them off and I don't think Neville Southall was too happy!

'I broke the great Dixie Dean's record, and it was another FA Cup winner's medal for me. We won it for the people of Hillsborough'

Celebrating the winning goal with John Barnes after Everton pegged us back twice with Stuart McCall scoring both their goals

More FAVOURITE Shirts

1990 Kenny Dalglish Testimonial
A Salute To The King

Over 30,000 fans turned out for Kenny's testimonial against Real Sociedad in August 1990. I scored twice in a 3-1 win but it was all about saluting one of the greatest players in the club's history. I'm so privileged to have been able to play alongside Kenny. I was spoiled to be honest and I wouldn't have got half as many goals without him as a strike partner.

1990 Liverpool Away
Silver Shirt With A Silver Lining

I really liked the silver away kits because they looked good and were different, but the shirts I won things in, like the European Cup, hold the best memories. The red Crown Paints and Candy ones remind me of Wembley and I don't think you can beat a red Liverpool shirt. Having said that, this reminds me of the club's last title win. It seems mad now looking back and thinking Liverpool haven't won the championship since. We had some good away performances in that shirt.

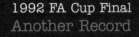

1991-1992 Liverpool Away
One To Forget

To be honest, I'm not sure why I've still hung on to this shirt as I don't think we won a game in it. The following season, adidas kept a similar design and the sponsors changed to Carlsberg. That shirt had better memories for me because I broke Roger Hunt's goalscoring record in it at Old Trafford. Come to think of it, I'm not sure what happened to that shirt now. I'll have to have another look in the loft.

1992 FA Cup Final
Another Record

It wasn't a classic season for us under Graeme Souness but we managed to finish on a high by beating Sunderland 2-0 at Wembley and this was the shirt I was wearing when I scored the second goal after Michael Thomas. People remember his goal more from that final, and rightly so, but on a personal level, it was my fifth goal in FA Cup finals at Wembley – which is still a record.

1993-1995 Gold Kit
Long And Short Sleeves

This is when kits started getting launched more often for commercial reasons and it caused a bit of controversy at the time. The badge changed again and the club added in the two Hillsborough flames.

This was the third kit. It had a golden yellow shirt with a black pattern in the fabric. Someone who knows about kits once told me it was the first time that adidas didn't have a logo as such and it was just their name on the shirt; it's not the sort of thing I'd notice.

It was around this time when they first started putting your name above your number, I loved that. I remember being sat on the coach that season and I saw someone going to the game with 'Rush 9' on the back of their shirt. Seeing someone wear your name makes you feel really proud – you want to go out and play well for them.

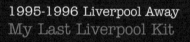

1995-1996 Liverpool Away
My Last Liverpool Kit

This isn't the actual shirt I wore in my final appearance for Liverpool against Manchester United in the 1996 FA Cup Final, but it's the one that I'll always associate with that game. Well this and the white suits! I knew it was my last game for Liverpool. I'd agreed to go to Leeds United and I knew I was going to be on the bench. It was built up to be one of the best games ever, but was most probably one of the worst games ever.

I came on at 0-0, but the ball touched me off a corner and fell to Eric Cantona who lashed it into the goal. I still blame Rob Jones for getting out the way of it on the line. If we had been winning I was expecting not to have got on the pitch, but to come on to lose in the final to Man United was so disappointing. I was thinking 'I'll never play in front of these supporters again' and that didn't sink in straight away.

1994 My Testimonial Shirt
A Fantastic Night At Anfield

I wore this shirt for my Anfield testimonial against Celtic in December 1994 and while I was never a player who tended to suffer from nerves in the dressing room, I was more tense that night than I can ever remember.

I wanted it to be a successful night, but more than that I was desperate to thank all the fans who attended – over 25,000 turned up including thousands from Glasgow – by scoring a goal.

Even though he was 43 and managing Blackburn, Kenny Dalglish agreed to play for some of the game and I'm glad he did. We were 5-0 up with 10 minutes to play and I hadn't scored, but when Kenny hit a shot I followed it in – just like the old days – and was on hand to put it in the net after Packie Bonner spilled it. There was a huge roar and I was very relieved to have scored!

World Class
INTERNATIONALS

Wales v Germany
Euro '96 qualifier, April 26, 1995

My winning goal against world champions Germany at the old Cardiff Arms Park in 1991 is probably my most famous for Wales, but I swapped this shirt when we played them in the qualifying campaign for Euro '96.

We drew 1-1 in Dusseldorf, Dean Saunders scored, but lost 2-1 in Cardiff. After the game in Germany I was approached by Jurgen Klinsmann, who was at Tottenham at the time, and he asked if I'd like to swap with him.

It is now framed and hung up on my wall close to Marco van Basten's. They wouldn't have been a bad strike partnership.

JURGEN
KLINSMANN

Netherlands v Wales
World Cup qualifier, Sep 14, 1988

Less than a month after I had returned to Liverpool from Juventus, I was on international duty for Wales as the qualifying campaign for the 1990 World Cup in Italy kicked off. We couldn't have had a tougher start.

We had to go to Amsterdam to face Holland who had won the European Championships that summer playing some fantastic football.

I captained the team and we battled really hard that night only to lose 1-0 when Ruud Gullit scrambled home a winner with just seven minutes to play.

When the full-time whistle went, the legendary Marco van Basten, who had scored that stunning volley against Russia in the Euro '88 final, came over and asked me to swap shirts!

I was quite taken aback – Marco van Basten wanted my Wales shirt! He was an incredible goalscorer, the best striker in the world at the time, and I've now got his shirt framed and hung on my wall at home. It isn't the only one, either…

MARCO
VAN BASTEN

1990-1992 Wales Away
Me And Deano

I'm not quite sure what Umbro's designers were thinking when they came up with this design, but we wore it during our Euro '92 qualifying campaign. I'm not entirely sure, but I think this may be the actual shirt I wore for the 1-1 draw in Belgium in March 1991.

Dean Saunders scored for us that night and he ended up with me at Liverpool a few months later as Graeme Souness wanted us to reproduce our international strike partnership at club level.

Unfortunately it didn't work out as I suffered an Achilles tendon injury that summer, which I put down to the drastically different training methods Graeme introduced, and when I returned I suffered a cartilage injury that ruled me out for almost three months. We only scored in the same game once – the Charity Shield against Leeds in August 1992 – and less than a month later ,Graeme sold Deano to Aston Villa. Had we both been fit for the full season, it could've worked out differently.

1992-1994 Wales Home
Devastated To Lose To Romania

I don't know which game this was from, but we wore this kit for our World Cup qualifying campaign for USA '94. We had to beat Romania in Cardiff in our final game to qualify. We lost 2-1, the first time we'd been beaten at the Arms Park in years and, as I've said before, that devastated us.

For me, from a Wales point of view, it was the worst time of my life. We genuinely thought we were going to go to America for the World Cup after a couple of near misses in the 1980s.

Romania had a fella called Hagi, who wasn't a bad player. He scored, Romania qualified and got to the quarter-finals of the World Cup. I was so devastated I actually thought about quitting international football because I knew my time was running out and when I went back to Liverpool I just didn't perform for two or three weeks.

Normally, when you don't perform well, you don't know the reason why, but I knew it was the after-effects of not qualifying for the World Cup.

Playing For KEEPS

KEVIN RATCLIFFE

EVERTON

Liverpool v Everton
Milk Cup Final, March 25/28, 1984

The first all-Merseyside final at Wembley was in the Milk Cup in 1984. We won 1-0 after a replay at Maine Road and my Welsh international team-mate Kevin Ratcliffe was marking me for both games.

While we were great friends off the pitch, I was determined to put one over him on it! Kev did me twice in the opening exchanges so when we went up for a high cross, I happened to catch him on the nose with my arm, only to hit him a bit harder than intended. Next thing, he's coughing up blood and struggling to breathe! When he got his breath back he charged towards me… and we both ended up laughing!

We swapped shirts after the game and we're still good mates now.

Scotland v Wales
Home Nations Cup, 1982/1984

We played Scotland at Hampden Park in the old Home Nations Cup in 1982 and 1984. It was after one of those games that I ended up with this shirt belonging to Kenny Dalglish. Before the game, I'd bumped into Kenny and he said to me that we should swap shirts afterwards, which was a really nice gesture from him.

I've got some great memories of Hampden Park as I not only made my Welsh schoolboy and full international debuts there, but scored the winner in a qualifying match for the 1986 World Cup. It was ground I enjoyed playing at.

KENNY DALGLISH

SCOTLAND

Bayern Munich v Liverpool
European Cup semi-final,
2nd Leg, April 22, 1981

KURT NIEDERMAYER

It's quite incredible really but my second game at Anfield for Liverpool – and just my fourth in total – was the 1981 European Cup semi-final against Bayern Munich.

David Johnson was injured so Bob Paisley picked me to start. We drew 0-0 on the night and for the second leg David was fit again, so I was back on the bench. Kenny got injured early on and I thought I might be brought on, but Bob went for Howard Gayle and he had a stormer.

Ray Kennedy's goal put us through on away goals in Munich and although I didn't get on, I ended up swapping shirts with their number 10, Kurt Niedermayer, at full-time.

France v Wales
International Friendly, June 2, 1982

We travelled to Toulouse to play France in the summer of '82 because the French wanted a pre-World Cup warm-up game against British opposition as their first game in Spain was to be against England.

It backfired on them though because I scored the only goal of the game, my second for Wales, and they got booed off, which must have hurt their confidence. They ended up losing to England 3-1.

At full-time I swapped shirts with the great Michel Platini, who signed for Juventus that summer. Little did I know at the time that I'd end up following him to Turin in 1987, although I never played with him as he retired a couple of months earlier, aged 32.

MICHEL PLATINI

Wales v Spain
World Cup Qualifier, April 30, 1985

Wales narrowly missed out on qualifying for the 1986 World Cup in Mexico, but beating Spain 3-0 at the Racecourse in Wrexham was definitely a highlight.

I scored our first and last goals that night – a tap-in and a one-on-one – but everyone remembers it for Mark Hughes smashing a fantastic scissors-kick volley into the top corner.

Afterwards I swapped shirts with Spain's number 5, Goicoechea Andoni, who was famously known as 'the Butcher of Bilbao'. He was the guy who broke Maradona's ankle in 1983 and got a 16-game ban, but I don't think he enjoyed playing against me.

Two months after that incident, he was marking me when Liverpool beat Atletico Bilbao 1-0 in Spain in the European Cup and I scored the only goal.

GOICOECHEA ANDONI

THE BOY DONE GOOD!

I've been lucky enough to win a lot of medals and caps during my career. Here are some personal favourites from my collection...

DEESIDE PRIMARY
CHAMPIONS OF WALES
1972-73
IAN RUSH

Deeside Primary Champions Trophy

I was only 11 years old when I got my hands on this trophy and it's fair to say we won it in style.

Deeside Primary Schools reached the final of the Welsh Yeoman Shield in 1973 where we faced Newport, who were the holders.

After winning the first leg in South Wales 3-1, in which I scored, we played the second leg in Queensferry and I netted twice in an 8-1 win.

As you'll see, it wasn't the only trophy to end up in the Rush household down the years, with the Flintshire Under-13s Champions Of Wales 1974/75 another in my collection.

Flintshire
Under 13
Champions
Of Wales
1974-75
Ian Rush

Welsh Pride

My dad was such a proud Welshman that it was my first international caps rather than any Liverpool shirts that he got framed and hung on the wall. I even scored the winner on my Welsh schoolboys debut away to Scotland in 1977 and funnily enough Scotland were the opponents again when I made my full international debut in 1980. Knowing how proud he was, I gave both of these caps to my dad to thank him for all he had done for me.

Youth International
Debut Cap. 9th April, 1977

Welsh Schools Football Association

This cap was presented to Ian Rush on his selection for
Wales Schools versus Scotland at Perth
~ 9th April 1977 ~
Scotland 0 - Wales 1 (Scorer Ian Rush)

Full International
Debut Cap. 21st May, 1980

Welsh Football Association

This cap was presented to Ian Rush
on his full international debut for Wales
against Scotland at Hampden Park
~ 21st May 1980 ~

1981 League Cup Winner's Medal

There can't be too many players who make their second appearance for Liverpool in a cup final and end up with a winner's medal, but that's what happened to me in 1981. I hadn't even made my home debut at Anfield at that stage!

We beat West Ham 2-1 to win the League Cup at Villa Park and the papers said it looked like I'd been playing alongside Kenny Dalglish for years.

RUSH TO STARDOM

THAT was the week that was for Flint's super soccer hero, Ian Rush, who in the space of just a few days shot into the limelight with his performances for Liverpool.

It all began when 19 - year - old Ian, of 51 Woodfield Avenue, was selected to play in Liverpool's League Cup final clash against West Ham United at Villa Park and put in a faultless performance in the 2-1 victory.

Then two days later, Ian turned out for the Reds again in a League match at Anfield and again put in an impressive performance in Liverpool's 3-0 victory over Stoke City.

An obviously delighted Ian said after his League Cup final appearance: "The whole atmosphere was just great. It was my biggest ever game and when the crowds started to chant my name it was fantastic.

"I had only known a few hours before that I was to play and I was pleased with the way my game went on the night. My ambition now is to try and establish a regular place in the first team having tasted what's it's like in the big time".

■ Ian shows his medal to his brothers, Gerald, Graham, Peter and Stephen.

Proud Ian shows off cup medal

Flint's Ian Rush won his first cup medal on Wednesday when he gave a faultless performance for Liverpool in their 2-1 League Cup final win over West Ham United at Villa Park.

The 19-year-old striker was back at his home 51 Woodfield Avenue, Flint yesterday proudly showing his parents Doris and Francis the gold medal.

Along with millions of other television viewers Ian's family watched him parade around Villa Park with the League Cup. Wearing Liverpool's coveted number nine shirt. Ian was drafted in as a last minute replacement to play alongside the great Kenny Dalglish.

Ian, in only his second full match for Liverpool since he signed from Chester for £300,000, took his opportunity magnificently. Twice he came close to scoring, but more importantly he fitted in with Liverpool team and looked as if he had been playing alongside Dalglish for years.

"It was a magnificent atmosphere and a great game to play in. I felt as I had played well and lot of people came up to me after the game and congratulated me on a good performance, he said.

Ian, who attended St. Richard Gwyn School, joined Chester two years ago.

He had since earned a full Welsh international cap although he is not in the squad at the moment.

Doing A Double Double In 1982 And 1983

The league and FA Cup double Liverpool won in 1986 is the most famous, but people forget we did doubles in 1982 and 1983 as well.

I scored 30 goals in 1981/82, my breakthrough season at Anfield, and won my first Division One championship medal.

We also retained the League Cup, beating Spurs, and as you've read, I scored my first Wembley goal for Liverpool in the process. For it to come against our former goalie, Ray Clemence, was incredible.

In 1982/83, Bob Paisley's last as manager, we did exactly the same double again!

I scored 31 goals that year, including another one against Clem at Wembley in the Charity Shield, and we beat Man United in the newly-renamed Milk Cup final.

What I really wanted to add to my collection next were European Cup and FA Cup winning medals.

1984 European Cup Final Medal

Not only is it my favourite away trip, but my 1984 European Cup winner's medal is also my favourite medal. It was a dream come true to be part of a Liverpool team that were Champions of Europe.

1984 League Winner's Medal

I scored 32 league goals this season, my best ever total, as we won our first championship under Joe Fagan. Three of them came at Villa Park – one of my most famous hat-tricks in a Liverpool shirt.

1984 Milk Cup Winner's Medal

By the time the 1983/84 season finished, I couldn't remember what it was like not to win the League Cup! We won it for a fourth time on the bounce by beating Everton in a replay, but for once I didn't score against the Blues. I put that right a few years later.

'I was the first British player to win the European Golden Boot, it has pride of place in my home'

NICO CLAESEN

MARCO VAN BASTEN

AJAX

CROWN PAINS

1984 European Golden Boot

I was the first British player to win the European Golden Boot. In other countries, Holland or somewhere like that, someone would come through and score 40 or 50 goals.

I always remember Franz Beckenbauer saying no-one will win the Golden Boot playing in England or Germany because it is too competitive and the league is too hard.

I scored 32 league goals and it is the league goals that count. Second was Marco van Basten and Nico Claesen, who later came to Tottenham.

I was very lucky in a way because

»

SOULIER D'OR 1984
RUSH (Liverpool)

Past European Golden Boot Winners

1967–68	Eusébio	Benfica	Portuguese Primeira Liga	43
1968–69	Petar Zhekov	CSKA Sofia	Bulgarian A PFG	36
1969–70	Gerd Müller	Bayern Munich	German Bundesliga	38
1970–71	Josip Skoblar	Marseille	French Ligue 1	44
1971–72	Gerd Müller	Bayern Munich	German Bundesliga	40
1972–73	Eusébio	Benfica	Portuguese Primeira Liga	40
1973–74	Héctor Yazalde	Sporting CP	Portuguese Primeira Liga	46
1974–75	Dudu Georgescu	Dinamo Bucharest	Romanian Divizia A	33
1975–76	Sotiris Kaiafas	Omonia Nicosia	Cypriot First Division	39
1976–77	Dudu Georgescu	Dinamo Bucharest	Romanian Divizia A	47
1977–78	Hans Krankl	Rapid Vienna	Austrian Bundesliga	41
1978–79	Kees Kist	AZ Alkmaar	Dutch Eredivisie	34
1979–80	Erwin Vandenbergh	Lierse	Belgian League	39
1980–81	Georgi Slavkov	PFC Botev Plovdiv	Bulgarian A PFG	31
1981–82	Wim Kieft	Ajax	Dutch Eredivisie	32
1982–83	Fernando Gomes	Porto	Portuguese Primeira Liga	36
1983–84	Ian Rush	Liverpool	English First Division	32
1984–85	Fernando Gomes	Porto	Portuguese Primeira Liga	39
1985–86	Marco van Basten	Ajax	Dutch Eredivisie	37
1986–87	Rodion Cămătaru	Dinamo Bucharest	Romanian Divizia A	44
1986–87	Toni Polster	Austria Wien	Austrian Bundesliga	39
1987–88	Tanju Çolak	Galatasaray	Süper Lig	39
1988–89	Dorin Mateuţ	Dinamo Bucharest	Romanian Divizia A	43
1989–90	Hugo Sánchez	Real Madrid	Spanish La Liga	38
1989–90	Hristo Stoichkov	CSKA Sofia	Bulgarian A PFG	38
1990–91	Darko Pančev	Red Star	Yugoslav First League	34
1991–92	Ally McCoist	Rangers	Scottish Premier Division	34
1992–93	Ally McCoist	Rangers	Scottish Premier Division	34
1993–94	David Taylor	Porthmadog	League of Wales	43
1994–95	Arsen Avetisyan	Homenetmen	Armenian Premier League	39
1995–96	Zviad Endeladze	Margveti	Georgian Umaglesi Liga	40
1996–97	Ronaldo	Barcelona	Spanish La Liga	34
1997–98	Nikos Machlas	Vitesse	Dutch Eredivisie	34
1998–99	Mário Jardel	Porto	Portuguese Primeira Liga	36
1999–20	Kevin Phillips	Sunderland	English Premier League	30
2000–01	Henrik Larsson	Celtic	Scottish Premier League	35
2001–02	Mário Jardel	Sporting CP	Portuguese Primeira Liga	42
2002–03	Roy Makaay	Deportivo La Coruña	Spanish La Liga	29
2003–04	Thierry Henry	Arsenal	English Premier League	30
2004–05	Thierry Henry	Arsenal	English Premier League	25
2004–05	Diego Forlán	Villarreal	Spanish La Liga	25
2005–06	Luca Toni	Fiorentina	Italian Serie A	31
2006–07	Francesco Totti	Roma	Italian Serie A	26
2007–08	Cristiano Ronaldo	Manchester United	English Premier League	31
2008–09	Diego Forlán	Atlético Madrid	Spanish La Liga	32
2009–10	Lionel Messi	Barcelona	Spanish La Liga	34
2010–11	Cristiano Ronaldo	Real Madrid	Spanish La Liga	40
2011–12	Lionel Messi	Barcelona	Spanish La Liga	50

Van Basten scored something like 30 and he'd been injured for something like half the season in Holland. It was the year we did the treble and I think I most probably came of age.

I was presented with this in Paris and it has pride of place in my trophy collection because to win the Golden Boot is incredible.

I say I scored 50 goals that year because I got 32 league goals, 16 in the cups and three in the Screen Sport Super Cup. I then got the penalty in the European Cup final so people say I got 49, but I say 50.

This is a favourite accolade because to score 32 league goals in a season is no mean feat.

IAN
RUSH
LIVERPOOL

'Franz Beckenbauer once said that no one from the English league would win the Golden Boot because it was too competitive'

1984 Football Writers' Association Footballer Of The Year

Stanley Matthews, Tom Finney, Bobby Moore, George Best, Kevin Keegan, Kenny Dalglish – some of the greatest names in football have won the Football Writers' Association Footballer of the Year award and in 1984 I added my name to the list. I was the first ever Welshman to receive the honour – only Neville Southall has done it since – and as you can see, it is a very distinctive trophy.

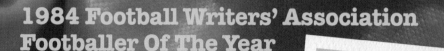

F.W.A.
FOOTBALLER OF THE YEAR 1983-84
IAN RUSH
LIVERPOOL & WALES

World Club Championship Medals

There aren't too many losers' medals in my trophy cabinet, but these are some of them. We travelled to Tokyo in 1981 to face Flamengo in the World Club Championship but we struggled against the Brazilians, who included the famous Zico (pictured below) and lost 3-0. We then repeated the jouney in 1984 and lost 1-0 to Independiente of Argentina. They are certainly some of the more unusual medals in my collection.

TOYOTA EUROPEAN SOUTH AMERICAN CUP

DECEMBER 13th..
1 9 8 1
NATIONAL STADIUM
TOKYO JAPAN
PRESENTED
By
TOYOTA

1986 League Winner's Medal

For quite a while it looked like Everton would run away with the title, but my late winner at Tottenham in March that I talked about earlier set us off on a run in which we won 11 and drew one of our final 12 games, enabling us to snatch the championship on the final day with a 1-0 win at Chelsea. As you know, it was Kenny who scored the winning goal at Stamford Bridge. I netted 33 goals that season, but not many managers can claim to have got the league winner themselves!

1986 FA Cup
Winner's Medal

1986 was incredible from an individual point of view. It was the year we did the league and FA Cup double and to beat Everton 3-1 at Wembley, after being 1-0 down at half-time in my first FA Cup final, was special. I scored two of the goals and to this day people remind me of the one which hit the camera in the back of the net!

1989 FA Cup Winner's Medal

When we walked out at Wembley in '89 we didn't know which was the Liverpool end and which was the Everton end. It was red and blue all around, Merseyside united. When the fans were singing 'Merseyside, Merseyside, Merseyside' – and sitting on the bench, I could really hear it – it was incredible. Liverpool and Everton supporters showed Merseyside at its best after Hillsborough. This was my first FA Cup final since returning from Juventus.

1990 League Winner's Medal

If anyone had told me Liverpool would not win another league championship after 1990 I wouldn't have believed them, but sadly that is how things turned out. This was my fifth league winners medal with the Reds and I was pleased with my form that year, scoring 26 times in total.

1980-81

Welsh International Retirement Cap

I retired from international football in 1996 and to mark it, the Welsh FA gave me this special yellow cap with the dates of my international career, 1980 to 1996, and the number of caps that I won on it. I think I'm right in saying you had to make 50 appearances or more to get one of these caps from the Welsh FA, but they don't present it to you until you have retired so they can put your final number of caps on it. I'm proud to have made 73 appearances for my country and my 28 goals for Wales is a record I am also very proud of.

GORAU·CHWARAE·CYD·CHWARAE

IAN RUSH
73
1980-1996

1995 – 96

1982-83

1988 – 89

1996 Awarded The MBE

A lot of my Liverpool goals were MBD – made by Dalglish – but in 1996 I was proud to visit Buckingham Palace with my wife Tracy and my two sons to collect an MBE from the Queen. She even said to me 'you've been playing for Liverpool for a long time now.' I know she likes the horses, but maybe she's a secret Red?

1984 PFA Player Of The Year

I'm proud to say that I was named as PFA Player of the Year in 1984, an award that meant a lot to me coming from my fellow professionals.

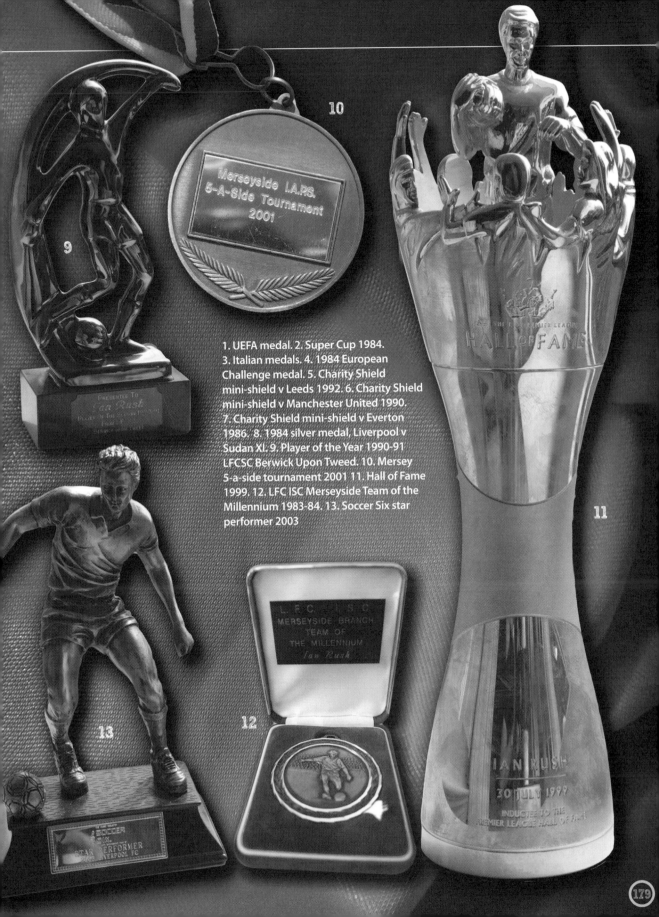

1. UEFA medal. 2. Super Cup 1984.
3. Italian medals. 4. 1984 European
Challenge medal. 5. Charity Shield
mini-shield v Leeds 1992. 6. Charity Shield
mini-shield v Manchester United 1990.
7. Charity Shield mini-shield v Everton
1986. 8. 1984 silver medal, Liverpool v
Sudan XI. 9. Player of the Year 1990-91
LFCSC Berwick Upon Tweed. 10. Mersey
5-a-side tournament 2001 11. Hall of Fame
1999. 12. LFC ISC Merseyside Team of the
Millennium 1983-84. 13. Soccer Six star
performer 2003

14. 1987 Runners-up League Trophy.
15. Robinson's Barley Water Young Player of the Month, October 1982.
16. BBC Radio Merseyside Special Award goblet 1983-84. 17. Football League medal box. 18. Welsh Sports Personality of the Year runner-up 1992. 19. Football League Legend 100 League Legends.
20. All Star Award Winner 1991. 21.Man of the Match v Manchester City, Fairhurst Computer Systems, November 24, 1990. 23. Silver Coca-Cola Bottle Manager of the Month 2004. 24. Various figures presented. 25 Young Player of the Year 1982

ALL YOU NEED IS
RUSH

So, you've had a look at some of my memorabilia from my playing days, now let me tell you about some of the things I used to get up to off the pitch and how I keep myself entertained these days...

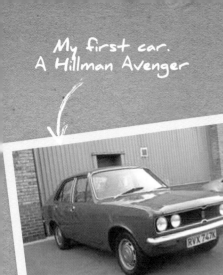
My first car.
A Hillman Avenger

Renault
Fuego

The hottest shape on the road.

FUEGO

RENAULT FUEGO
2-LITRE

My Love Of Cars

I bought my first car from my brother for
£200. It was a Hillman Avenger – a dark
green one – and sometimes I had to open
the bonnet to start the engine!

I passed my test when I was 17, although
I was driving when I was 14! I had an
Austin Allegro when I'd been at Chester
for about three months and there was a
lad who used to play for Chester, Alan
Tarbuck, who set up a car sales business
and he managed to sell me an Allegro on
which the roof came down. I still had that
when I went to Liverpool, but obviously
bought a new car after that – a Morris of
some sort from the local dealers in Flint.

I always loved cars. I used to have a
black Renault Fuego and then, even
worse, a black Porsche. Can you imagine
what they thought when I drove into Flint
in a black Porsche? I wasn't too popular!

There was also a red Porsche I had with
a RUSH 1 licence plate – me and Mark
Hughes both had the same car because
we had the same agent. Let's just say you
learn from these things!

My favourite cars are BMWs, to tell
you the truth. The Six Series
are great. I've got used
to them.

ALLEGRO

Austin
Allegro

I'm a pasta man. The baked beans story was a load of rubbish

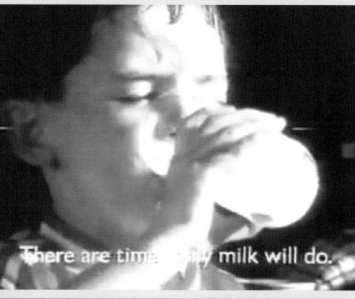

There are time...ly milk will do.

Accrington Stanley... Who are they?

What I Like To Eat And Drink

One thing I've always had is milk. It's funny saying that because of the advert, but I've always had it. The funny thing with that advert was that the kid who says 'Accrington Stanley, who are they?' was originally meant to say 'Arsenal, who are they', but Arsenal objected to it!

When Accrington Stanley came back into the Football League they wanted to re-do the advert, but the lad who starred in it is now an actor and refused to do it.

His real accent is very posh and apparently it annoys him that people still say 'exacctttly' in a Scouse accent to him now. At least that's the story I was told.

It originally came about because the milk people got in touch with my agent and asked permission to use my name. We came to an agreement and it ended up winning advert of the year! My sons actually Googled the advert the other day and were watching it.

Going back to food and drink, I used to love a steak in my Chester days because we didn't have it very often when I was younger. Cliff Sears would take us for some lovely meals.

When I went to Italy there was a story written about me loving baked beans, with the press saying I'd be taking loads of baked beans to Italy with me, which was a load of rubbish. What I did get into in

184

Italy was pasta, and Italian is my favourite food now. I love pasta and a glass of wine.

When you have a glass of wine over there, you also have water with it and it makes a lot of difference. Before that I used to drink beer. In Italy, if you have six bottles of wine, they see it as being okay, but if you have one pint of beer, they say you've got a drink problem!

When I was at Liverpool, we'd get fish and chips on Fridays! My pre-match meal at Liverpool was steak and beans, so it was completely different to in Italy.

How it was in Italy in 1987 is how it is in England today. They were way ahead of us although I'd say the Premier League is the best in the world now and a lot of foreign players come here, especially with all the money that's about.

You never know what to expect in English football and even though people come in and want to change things, the spirit of British people always shines through.

Whether you're Northern Irish, Welsh, English or Scottish, that's one thing you never want to lose because it's the one thing the Europeans never take into account when they come and play here. The will to win of the British is the best in the world.

Sureshot Ian Rush, the most consistent goalscorer in the First Division for the past few years, isn't joking when he says strikers are like gunfighters.

The 22-year-old Welsh international with the razor reflexes and hawk-eyed accuracy leads Liverpool's attack with a consistency that bears all the hallmarks of a "killer".

Feared throughout Europe, he is the subject of a growing number of "wanted" posters in many parts of the Continent.

Hardly surprising then that when he wants to get away from the pressures of football and his never-ending showdowns with top defenders and goalkeepers, Rush turns to ... guns!

"It's not as sinister as it sounds," he says, "Though I must admit that there are some strong comparisons to be made.

"Goalscoring is about accuracy, having a good eye for a chance and the nerve to finish first time, without hesitation, mercy or any lingering doubts about your ability.

"I imagine the Wild West gunfighters were the same — they could not afford any self-doubt, nor could they allow any nerves to set in. They were quick, accurate and capable of finishing with the first shot.

"In my case I need something that gets me right away from big crowds and my profession. Everybody needs to relax now and again and I'm no exception.

"Many players enjoy a round of golf. I do, but not to the same extent. To be honest, the weather often makes it impossible to play.

"Then a friend invited me along to the shooting range at Sealand, Chester, and introduced me to clay pigeon shooting. I soon got the hang of the rifle and found I enjoyed the challenge of mastering a whole new form of leisure activity.

"I took Jan Molby along and he found he enjoyed the sport as much as me.

"The great thing is that every couple of years they have a big event day at Sealand — members of the Royal Family usually attend — and they get up a team of footballers who shoot to take on another team. Top names such as Jack Charlton are regulars."

Jan Molby joins his Liverpool team-mate as Ian sharpens his aim in preparation for Newcastle's visit to Anfield this Saturday.

Liverpool's master marksman shoots for his life~ and fun

IAN RUSH

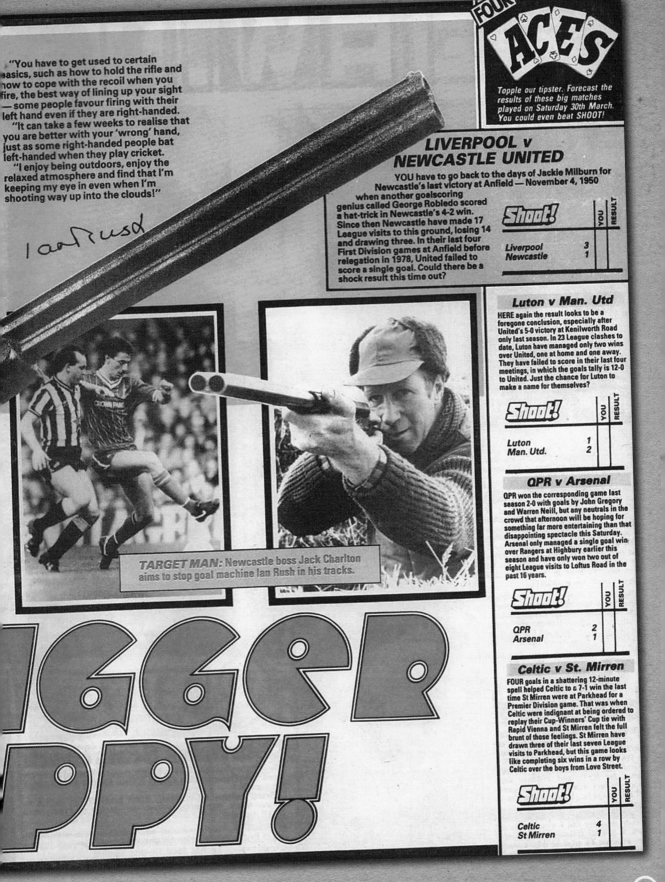

"You have to get used to certain basics, such as how to hold the rifle and how to cope with the recoil when you fire, the best way of lining up your sight — some people favour firing with their left hand even if they are right-handed.

"It can take a few weeks to realise that you are better with your 'wrong' hand, just as some right-handed people bat left-handed when they play cricket.

"I enjoy being outdoors, enjoy the relaxed atmosphere and find that I'm keeping my eye in even when I'm shooting way up into the clouds!"

Ian Rush

TARGET MAN: Newcastle boss Jack Charlton aims to stop goal machine Ian Rush in his tracks.

Topple our tipster. Forecast the results of these big matches played on Saturday 30th March. You could even beat SHOOT!

LIVERPOOL v NEWCASTLE UNITED

YOU have to go back to the days of Jackie Milburn for Newcastle's last victory at Anfield — November 4, 1950 when another goalscoring genius called George Robledo scored a hat-trick in Newcastle's 4-2 win. Since then Newcastle have made 17 League visits to this ground, losing 14 and drawing three. In their last four First Division games at Anfield before relegation in 1978, United failed to score a single goal. Could there be a shock result this time out?

Shoot!

	YOU	RESULT
Liverpool	3	
Newcastle	1	

Luton v Man. Utd

HERE again the result looks to be a foregone conclusion, especially after United's 5-0 victory at Kenilworth Road only last season. In 23 League clashes to date, Luton have managed only two wins over United, one at home and one away. They have failed to score in their last four meetings, in which the goals tally is 12-0 to United. Just the chance for Luton to make a name for themselves?

Shoot!

	YOU	RESULT
Luton	1	
Man. Utd.	2	

QPR v Arsenal

QPR won the corresponding game last season 2-0 with goals by John Gregory and Warren Neill, but any neutrals in the crowd that afternoon will be hoping for something far more entertaining than that disappointing spectacle this Saturday. Arsenal only managed a single goal win over Rangers at Highbury earlier this season and have only won two out of eight League visits to Loftus Road in the past 16 years.

Shoot!

	YOU	RESULT
QPR	2	
Arsenal	1	

Celtic v St. Mirren

FOUR goals in a shattering 12-minute spell helped Celtic to a 7-1 win the last time St Mirren were at Parkhead for a Premier Division game. That was when Celtic were indignant at being ordered to replay their Cup-Winners' Cup tie with Rapid Vienna and St Mirren felt the full brunt of those feelings. St Mirren have drawn three of their last seven League visits to Parkhead, but this game looks like completing six wins in a row by Celtic over the boys from Love Street.

Shoot!

	YOU	RESULT
Celtic	4	
St Mirren	1	

Keeping Up Appearances With Ex-Team-mates

I still keep in touch with quite a few old team-mates, especially with having the former players matches now. I'm still pretty close with Ronnie Whelan, Jan Molby, Michael Thomas and John Barnes.

All of them, as well as Paul Ince, live quite close to me so we still meet up and have a laugh. We always enjoyed each other's company, that's what it's all about.

The former players enjoy it more now than when they were playing. I also still see Robbie Fowler quite a bit, plus Michael Owen and Didi Hamann.

They Loved Life At Liverpool And Ended Up Staying For Good

I think it just goes to show how much they loved the club and what it was all about. Lads like Jan Molby, Michael Thomas and John Barnes loved the place so much that they're still here.

People talk about what Michael Thomas did for Arsenal more than Liverpool, but he always says to me that Liverpool was the better club.

Relaxing Away From Football

I loved horse racing and played a bit of golf and snooker during my playing days. I remember going out playing snooker in Liverpool with Ronnie Whelan and we'd see John Parrott playing in the same place. I've also always loved holidays. When you're playing with the same people for eight or nine months a year, you just want to get away for a bit of sun, and recharge your batteries for the next season.

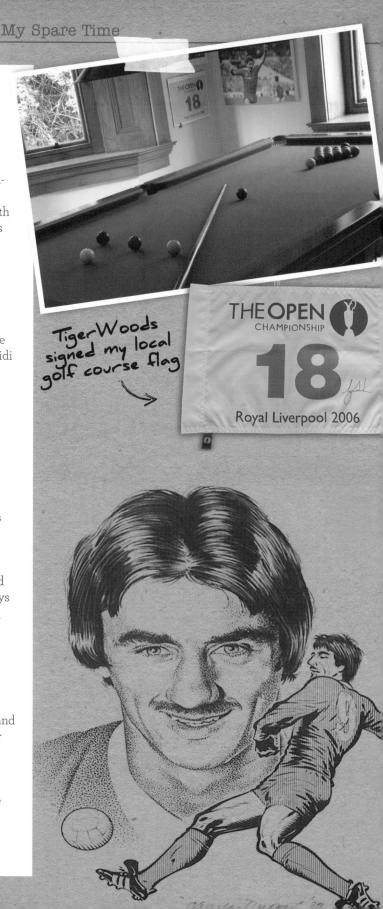

TigerWoods signed my local golf course flag

THE OPEN CHAMPIONSHIP
18
Royal Liverpool 2006

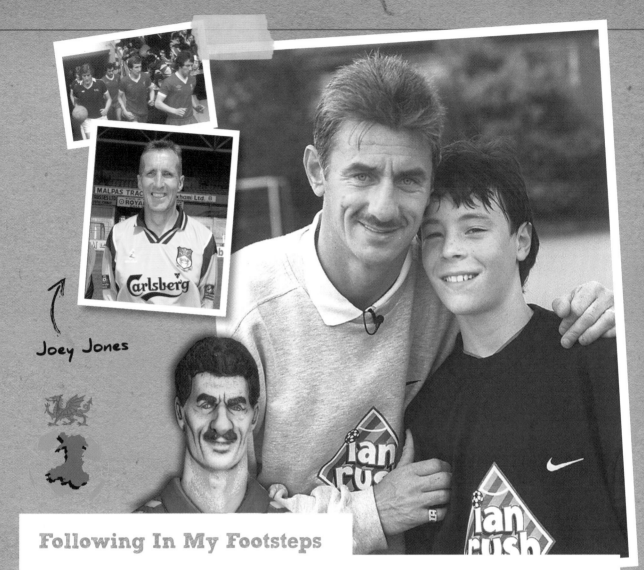

Joey Jones

Following In My Footsteps

My eldest son, Jonathan, has always enjoyed his football. He played in the League of Wales and actually turns out for Flint now, along with two or three of my nephews. He loves doing that. He's scored some goals, too. He's 6ft 4ins and Joey Jones looked after him at Wrexham between the ages of 14 to 16.

Jon wanted to stay on at school and focus on his education. It was only when he went to university that he decided he wanted to get back into playing again and that's what he's done.

He's doing a sports industry degree now and has done a work placement for Liverpool.

The youngest one, Daniel, wants to be an architect. He was completely different. He

plays at right-back and is the type of lad who does just enough. He's one who just wants to play games, not practice and train, but the two of them are best of mates and play 5-a-side in midweek together.

I still go to Flint to watch Jon play and it gives me a great buzz when he scores.

I was watching him play for Cefn Druids, once, and at the end of the game someone said to him 'you're not as good as your dad'.

He turned around and said 'If I was as good as my dad do you think I'd be playing here?'

It was a great answer because there is a lot of pressure on them – that's just how football works.

As long as he enjoys it, good luck to him.

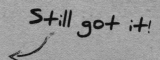

Still got it!

Staying In Shape

I'm very lucky in that I didn't get many bad injuries, only cartilage injuries.

I love playing and I'm going to continue as long as I can. When you're coaching as well, particularly the younger ones, you can demonstrate things to them. When I go to The Academy and can demonstrate what I'm saying, they love it. It's also great when you can join in and play with 15 and 16 year-olds. You've got to know when to stop, though!

My Liverpool Masters Team-mates Who Have Still 'Got It'

I like 11-a-side more than the Masters format. There are a lot of younger ones playing in that now, especially indoor – lads who are only 35 and who recently stopped playing.

For me, it's unbelievable to see people like Phil Neal still playing. He keeps himself fit. And then there's Jan – who doesn't need to run, he's still such a good passer of the ball.

John Barnes has put weight on, but you wouldn't want to play against him! They were super players and they still don't give the ball away now.

Liverpool haven't won the league since 1990 and if you look at the players who came through after that era – McAteer, Robbie, players like that – they never won the league because they were individuals rather than a team. We played as a team. Robbie and Steve McManaman were special players, but it's no co-incidence that they didn't win as much as we did in the 1980s.

When we play now at 11-a-side, we need runners like Jason McAteer, but we also know that they're going to give the ball away. You'll still see Alan Kennedy, Phil Neal and Jan all holding their positions now because they've got football brains.

It was how they were brought up at Liverpool.

5-a-side was the Liverpool way in training and it went all the way back to Shankly

Developing A Football Brain

Coaching can help, but I think that you've got to have it in you to really know football. Today, stats like ProZone and so on are used. That's great, but you still need a football brain.

One of the best players I ever played with was Ray Kennedy. When he went to left midfield, he didn't do much running, but no-one ever got past him, and he'd always be coming in at the far post to score goals. That's because he had a football brain.

It makes me laugh, now. Players like Robbie Savage will run around. Sav would be covering 20 miles, but what has he done? It's about having the right mixture of players, but you need players with football brains.

The Secret Behind Liverpool's Success

Team spirit, it's exactly what we had. We only played 5-a-sides in training. Coaches used to come and watch us in the 1980s and all they'd see was 5-a-side.

What they didn't know was the conditions of the 5-a-side. We'd play two-touch, or we'd all have to be in one half before we could score.

Ronnie Moran would dictate how training sessions were going. If it wasn't going well he'd say 'unless you up it now, you're all going running'. If training was going really well he wouldn't say anything.

It was the pace and the speed of the 5-a-side that was important. Joe Fagan and Ronnie Moran believed in it because it had been established by Bill Shankly and Bob Paisley.

Passing On What I've Learned At Liverpool

You can take all the Liverpool philosophy with you, but when I was manager at Chester, they were unable to do what I was asking because they were lesser players.

It's difficult coaching at the top, but believe me – it's a lot harder below that because you've got the same pressures, but with less money and lesser players. It's easier to coach better players. With lesser players you have to work harder.

You only have to tell a good player something once, maybe twice, before they take it on board. With others you have to tell them things more often because they'll do something and then forget it. That's the art of coaching.

'It's difficult coaching at the top, but believe me – it's a lot harder below that'

Rushie's Liverpool Timeline

April 1981
Tastes success with Liverpool for the first time in just his second appearance when selected to start the 2-1 League Cup final replay victory over West Ham United at Villa Park

April 1981
Makes his home debut for Liverpool in a 3-0 victory against Stoke City

April 1981
First appearance in European competition comes in the European Cup semi-final, first leg match versus Bayern Munich at Anfield

1980

1981

May 1980
Signs for Liverpool FC from Chester City at the age of 19 for £300,000, a world record transfer fee for a teenager at the time

May 1980
Scores his first goal in a Liverpool shirt for the Reserves during a 3-3 draw at Blackpool

December 1980
Handed his full Liverpool debut by Bob Paisley away to Ipswich Town, after Kenny Dalglish is ruled out through injury, which the Reds draw 1-1

May 1981
Misses out on a European Cup winner's medal after Howard Gayle is named on the bench ahead of him for the 1-0 final victory against Real Madrid in Paris

September 1981
Nets his first Liverpool goal, coming off the bench in the number 13 shirt to score in a 7-0 European Cup first round victory over Oulu Palloseura at Anfield

October 1981:
Opens his account in the League Cup with two strikes in a 5-0 win against Exeter City

October 1981
Leeds United are the victims as he scores his first league goals for Liverpool as the Yorkshire club are beaten 3-0 at Anfield

November 1981
Marks his Merseyside derby debut with a goal in a 3-1 victory against boyhood heroes Everton at Anfield

January 1982
Meadow Lane, Nottingham witnesses his first Liverpool hat-trick as the Reds rout Notts County 4-0 in the First Division

January 1982
Gets off the mark in the FA Cup for Liverpool with a double in a 4-0 success at Swansea's Vetch Field in the 3rd round

March 1982
On target in extra-time at Wembley as Liverpool beat Tottenham 3-1 to retain the newly re-named Milk Cup

March 1983
Picks up another Milk Cup winner's medal following a 2-1 win against Manchester United at Wembley

May 1983
Named as PFA Young Player of the Year

May 1983
Ends the season with another First Division medal and 31 goals, beating his 1981/82 total by one

January 1984
Strikes a famous hat-trick in a 3-1 victory over Aston Villa on an icy Villa Park pitch that is ranked by many Kopites as the finest Liverpool hat-trick of all time

March 1984
Receives a 4th League Cup winner's medal in four seasons after Everton are beaten 1-0 in a replay at Maine Road

April 1984
Nets his 100th Liverpool goal in a 3-3 draw with Leicester City at Filbert Street

April 1984
Scores twice away to Dinamo Bucharest to clinch Liverpool a place in the European Cup final in Rome

1982   1983   1984

May 1982
Picks up his first league winner's medal after Bob Paisley's side clinch the title with a 3-1 win against Tottenham

November 1982
Becomes the first player to net a hat-trick in a Merseyside derby at Goodison Park since Dixie Dean in 1931 when scoring four as Liverpool thrash the Blues 5-0

August 1982
Scores his second goal at Wembley for the Reds by netting the winner against FA Cup holders Tottenham in the Charity Shield

October 1983
Scores five goals in a 6-0 win at home to Luton after wetting his boots before kick-off, sparking a life-long superstition

May 1984
Adds a 3rd Division One winner's title to his list of honours after Joe Fagan's men get the point they need at Notts County to win the league

May 1984
Scores his 32nd league goal of the season (47th in total) against Norwich City, winning him the adidas European Golden Boot for the most goals netted in any of the top European divisions

May 1984
Named as PFA Player of the Year and Football Writers' Footballer of the Year

May 1984
Converts a penalty in the first ever European Cup final penalty shoot-out as Liverpool complete a treble by beating AS Roma on spot-kicks in their own back yard to become champions of Europe

Rushie's Timeline

May 1986
Celebrates winning a 4th championship as the Reds pip Everton to the title by beating Chelsea 1-0 at Stamford Bridge thanks to a goal from player-manager Kenny Dalglish

March 1987
Notches his 200th goal for the Reds when on target twice as QPR are beaten 2-1 at Anfield

May 1988
Returns to Anfield to play in Alan Hansen's testimonial against an England XI

March 1985
Makes his 200th appearance for the Reds during a 1-0 win against Nottingham Forest

May 1986
Scores twice at Wembley as Liverpool beat Everton 3-1 in the first all-Merseyside FA Cup final to clinch the club's only league and FA Cup double

April 1987
Liverpool lose for the first time when he scores as Arsenal come from behind to win the Littlewoods Cup final 2-1 at Wembley

August 1988
Stuns the world of football by re-signing for the Reds for £2.7 million after one season with Juventus

1985   1986   1987   1988

May 1985
Part of the Liverpool side that is beaten 1-0 by Juventus in the European Cup final at Heysel on a tragic night when 39 supporters of the Italian club lose their lives

September 1986
Nets another Goodison Park hat-trick as the Reds thrash the Blues 4-1 to clinch a 7-2 aggregate success in the Screen Sport Super Cup

May 1987
Scores his 40th goal of the campaign on the final day at Chelsea to leave Liverpool having netted 207 goals in 331 appearances

August 1988
Makes his second 'debut' for the club as a substitute in a 3-0 win away to Charlton Athletic

October 1988
On target for the first time since returning from Italy when netting in a 3-1 Littlewoods Cup win at Walsall

April 1989
Starts the FA Cup semi-final against Nottingham Forest on the bench but the game is abandoned after six minutes as 96 Liverpool supporters lose their lives at Hillsborough in British sport's worst stadium disaster

May 1990
On target against QPR at Anfield in a 2-1 victory that secures a record 18th league title for Liverpool FC

April 1992
Finally breaks his duck against Manchester United by opening the scoring in a 2-0 Anfield victory that hands the league title to Leeds United

May 1992:
Nets a record 5th FA Cup final goal at Wembley when scoring in a 2-0 success against Sunderland

1989   1990   1991   1992

May 1989
Comes off the bench to score twice to clinch a 3-2 FA Cup final success for Liverpool against Everton at Wembley with his first goal beating Dixie Dean's Merseyside derby goalscoring record

February 1991
Scores in a sensational 4-4 Merseyside derby FA Cup draw at Goodison Park, after which Liverpool boss Kenny Dalglish resigns

September 1992
Finds the net four times in a 6-1 European Cup Winners' Cup win against Apollon Limassol at Anfield to take his tally in Europe to 19 goals, breaking Roger Hunt's club record of 17

October 1992
Makes his 500th appearance for the Reds during a 1-0 Anfield win against Sheffield Wednesday

May 1989
Limps off 30 minutes into the final league game of the season against Arsenal in which the Reds narrowly miss out on the league championship after Michael Thomas strikes a last-minute winner to take the title to Highbury

October 1992
Breaks Roger Hunt's all-time scoring record of 286 for Liverpool by netting his first ever Premier League goal and first ever strike at Old Trafford in a 2-2 draw against Manchester United

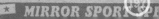

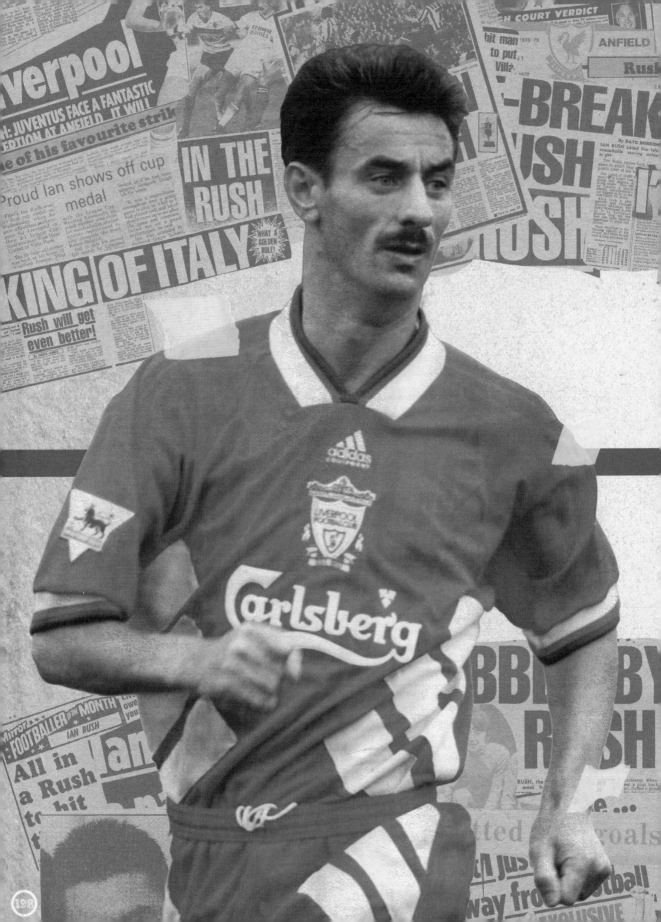

January 1996
Finds the net against Rochdale to break Denis Law's post-war record for the most goals scored in the FA Cup with what turns out to be his last goal at Anfield

April 1995
Picks up his first trophy as Liverpool captain, but his last as a Liverpool player, when the Reds beat Bolton 2-1 in the Coca-Cola Cup final at Wembley and in the process sets a new record for having the most League Cup winner's medals

March 1994
Nets a record 25th, and final, Merseyside derby goal as Liverpool beat Everton 2-1 in the last derby played in front of the old Spion Kop

May 1996
Scores his 346th and final Liverpool goal in a 2-2 draw at Maine Road that results in Manchester City being relegated

May 1993
Appointed as Liverpool captain by manager Graeme Souness

1993   1994   1995   1996

October 1993
Hits his 16th and final Liverpool hat-trick, one short of Roger Hunt's club record, in a 3-2 League Cup win at home to Ipswich Town

December 1994
A crowd of over 25,000 turn up at Anfield for his testimonial against Celtic which the Reds win 6-0

May 1987
Awarded an MBE in the New Year's honours list

May 1996
Makes his 660th and final Liverpool appearance in the 1-0 FA Cup final defeat to Manchester United before signing for Leeds United

ECLIPSING A LEGEND

To fully appreciate the magnitude of Rushie's goalscoring achievements at Anfield, you need to look at the table of club icons that the 346-goal marksman tops. Second on that list is a true great...'Sir' Roger Hunt

Call it the north-west rivalry or the fact they are the two most successful teams in English football's long history – when a Red scores against the Red Devils, it generally leads to pandemonium.

And that was certainly the case for Ian Rush when he netted against Sir Alex Ferguson's side on October 18th, 1992.

Not only did it give Liverpool a 2-0 lead following Don Hutchison's 23rd minute opener, it was also Rush's 287th strike for Liverpool, ensuring he now stood alone at the top of the Reds' goalscoring list.

He had finally broken Roger Hunt's 23-year record. Not bad for your first ever goal at Old Trafford.

Hunt was a fellow genius in front of the Kop, scoring 41 goals in the 1961-62 season before helping the Reds to the First Division title three seasons later, bagging a further 31 goals in that campaign.

He was not finished there either.

When Liverpool again won the title in 1965-66, Hunt scored 30 goals before going on to win the World Cup with England later that summer.

While Rush was still at primary school, Hunt was being unofficially knighted by the Kop and 'Sir' Roger Hunt showed the same classy touch in congratulating Rush as he had once done with a ball at his feet.

He said at the time: "It had to go some time and I'm delighted that it's been broken by such a great player.

"I used to blaze away all the time and score a lot of my goals from 20 yards or more, but I think Ian has scored more from close range, often by beating the offside trap or in one-on-one situations with the goalkeeper.

"He has always had a wonderful sense of anticipation and has been unbelievably quick off the mark.

"He stands comparison with the best of any era.

"When I scored my 41 goals, we were in the Second Division, and it was much easier to score."

Rush, of course, was not finished there as he bagged a further 59 goals in his Liverpool career to further cement his place as the club's greatest ever striker.

Liverpool's top 10 all-time goalscorers:

	Player	Goals	Games
1	Ian Rush	346	660
2	Roger Hunt	286	492
3	Gordon Hodgson	241	377
4	Billy Liddell	228	534
5	Robbie Fowler	183	369
6	Kenny Dalglish	172	515
7	Michael Owen	158	297
8	Steven Gerrard	154	611
9	Harry Chambers	151	339
10	Sam Raybould	130	226

* Table correct as of January 1, 2013

Overtaking a legend: Rush scores Liverpool's fourth goal and equals Roger Hunt's record against Chesterfield. Below: Rush in action against Manchester United, the game in which he surpassed Hunt's total

THE TOFFEES' TORMENTOR

The nature of football means that one man's hero is another man's villain.

And nobody on Merseyside has ever been as loved by the Reds and feared by the Blues as much as Ian Rush.

Twenty-five derby goals have ensured Rush's place in Merseyside folklore as he holds the record for the most strikes in English football's most passionate and iconic 90 minutes.

Nobody wants to lose the Merseyside derby. It makes Saturday night or Sunday afternoon miserable; it makes the workplace unbearable; it makes the banter and abuse of your family, friends and neighbours tough to stomach.

And Ian Rush is the best there has ever been at leaving the Toffees with a sticky ending.

While the likes of Manchester City and Coventry City – who both saw Rush score 15 times against them – had reason to curse his name, no side in the country felt Rushie's wrath more than Everton.

And what makes it worse is that he grew up an Evertonian!

The breadth of Rush's hoodoo over Liverpool's Stanley Park neighbours is astonishing.

After first scoring against Everton on November 7th, 1981 in a 3-1 win at Anfield, Liverpool's No.9 was still causing Everton nightmares on March 13th, 1994.

That is an enormously long time to be inflicting pain on anyone – never mind the side you supported as a boy.

In fact, Rush was Everton's No.1 tormentor for

4,510 days, which works out at exactly 12 years, four months and one week.

That is some record.

And to make matters worse, Rush became the leading scorer in the Merseyside derby – overtaking Everton's Dixie Dean – with his first goal against the Toffees at Wembley in the 1989 FA Cup final.

Talk about picking your moments.

And while any Reds legend would happily queue up to sing Rushie's praises, perhaps the last word should be left to a man he punished more than most during his career: Howard Kendall.

In fact the then Everton manager joked that he was delighted when Rush left for Juventus in 1987 so his side could get some peace and quiet.

Speaking to the Liverpool ECHO, Kendall said: "We can all sleep a little easier now. But at the same time he has given everyone a great deal of pleasure.

"Rush is clinical in front of goal in the mould of Jimmy Greaves. I always rated Jimmy as the finest goalscorer the English game has ever produced but Rush must be rated in the same bracket."

Praise from across the Park is not always the easiest to come by. But Rushie's eye for goal, statistics and knack of breaking Evertonian hearts is clearly respected across the city of Liverpool and beyond.

MY OTHER TEAMS

Most of my playing days were spent at Liverpool, but away from Anfield, I enjoyed running out for several other clubs and, of course, for Wales. I've also had the pleasure of passing on what I've learned from the game in a coaching and managerial capacity and still manage the odd appearance in Masters and charity games. All in all, I've had a pretty lively career...

Juventus

1987-1988

You've already read about my time at Juventus but one aspect of my season in Italy that I haven't mentioned is the Christmas fixture schedule. We were given two weeks off and I hated it. I just didn't like the idea of having a mid-season break.

That wasn't the only difference which frustrated me.

At Liverpool, the Christmas fancy dress party was a tradition we stuck to, and it was all part of encouraging a team spirit which I believed was the best in world. In Italy, players were more selfish and didn't feel bonding with team-mates was important.

Put it this way. There was no chance of me organising an event where we could all dress up as Batman and Robin in Turin.

When the Italian players heard what we were up to at Anfield, they couldn't get their head around it. I suppose it was just a different culture.

Me at Juventus in the pre-season team shot, I'm on the back row

Me and Mum posing with my Juventus shirt at her home

A commendable 1-1 draw in Germany during our World Cup qualifier in 1995

Scoring against the Czech Republic in a World Cup qualifier in 1993, but we ended up losing 2-1 and missing out on qualification, a real heartbreak

Wales

1980-1996

I was fortunate enough to live my dream. During my career I represented Wales 73 times and scored 28 goals for my national team.

We failed to qualify for a major international tournament during that time, which was frustrating.

But I remember once being asked if I regret not having been born English. I was incensed by this. I explained how I felt about being Welsh and how proud I was of my roots and country.

Leeds United

1996-1997

It was an emotional wrench to leave Liverpool, but I was realistic about my departure. It was time to move on and the fact a top club such as Leeds not only wanted me as a player but felt I was future management material, made the leaving of Liverpool easier for me.

A part of me wanted to prove Liverpool were wrong to let me go. So when they were due to visit Elland Road, I thought it would be perfect if I could score my first goal for Leeds against them. After all, I got my first league goal for Liverpool against Leeds, so it would be nice to do it the other way around. It never happened though, and Liverpool won 2-0.

Even though I had a loyalty to Leeds, I still felt a bond to Liverpool as a club and with its supporters, and still do.

Signing for Howard Wilkinson's Leeds side

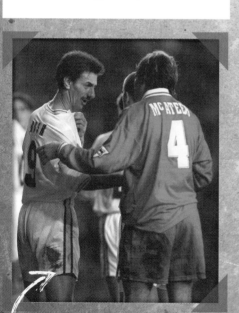

Playing against my old club seemed quite strange

Newcastle United

1997-1998

I was made to feel very welcome by the players at Newcastle and by those great Geordie fans, which helped me settle in straight away.

In October I scored in a 2-0 win against Hull City in the League Cup. The goal was an important milestone in my career as it meant I had equalled Sir Geoff Hurst's all-time individual record of 49 League Cup goals.

In January, Kenny Dalglish named me as a substitute for Newcastle's third round FA Cup tie at Everton. The game was goalless when I was called into action early in the second half. No sooner did I set foot on the pitch when I was greeted with a chorus of booing from the Everton fans, a reception that was repeated every time I touched the ball.

After 67 minutes, Keith Gillespie pulled the ball across goal and I slid it past Thomas Myhre. It proved to be my last goal in top-flight football. I thought it was fitting that it was against Everton.

My last top-flight goal, of course it had to come against Everton as we put them out of the FA Cup

Sheffield United

1998

I spent a month on loan at Sheffield United. My old Liverpool team-mate Nigel Spackman was manager. He had some injury problems in his squad and asked if I would help out for a few weeks, which I was only too pleased to do. I thought my brief spell at Bramall Lane would be my final bow, but not quite.

Equalling Sir Geoff Hurst's League Cup goalscoring record against Hull City

Wrexham

Player/Coach

1998-1999

In the summer of 1998 I received a call from former Liverpool full-back Joey Jones. Joey was the Wrexham coach and, knowing I was studying to become a coach, asked if I would consider going to Wrexham to help out in the development of their young players.

I went to Wrexham primarily to gain some practical experience of coaching, but their manager, Brian Flynn, persuaded me to sign as a player in the event of an emergency and I ended up playing 17 games for the first team.

I enjoyed my year with Wrexham, particularly my work on the coaching side. I might have stayed a little longer had I not been presented with the opportunity of another irresistible experience.

The top Australian club, Sydney Olympic, had offered me a short-term contract. I was 38 years-old but still felt fit enough to make a telling contribution to games for Sydney Olympic.

Learning the coaching game on the Wrexham touchline

Liverpool Striker Coach

2003-2004

While I was in Australia, I received a telephone call from Liverpool's Chief Executive, Rick Parry. He informed me that following the departure of Phil Thompson and Sammy Lee, Rafa Benitez was looking for someone to assist him with coaching. Rick asked if I would be interested and I had no hesitation in saying 'yes'.

The thought of returning to Liverpool and working alongside Rafa was my dream job. My elation, though, was to last only a matter of 48 hours, when Rick rang to tell me the club had appointed Alex Miller to help Rafa. Needless to say I was very disappointed, but in 2003 a dream came true when then-Liverpool manager Gerard Houllier contacted me and asked if I would return to Anfield to coach his strikers, who included Emile Heskey, Milan Baros, El Hadji Diouf and Michael Owen.

I found my work with the Liverpool strikers challenging but very rewarding.

Chester City

Manager

2004-2005

A lot of people seemed to think that before taking the job as Chester City manager I had been kicking my heels for five years doing nothing, just waiting for a job to turn up.

Nothing could be further from the truth. In fact, I had been coaching all over the world and working towards gaining my international coaching badges.

So, you can see that when I heard people thought I was coming into football management with no experience, I was a little annoyed and amused at the same time.

I took the Chester City job because I thought the time was right to take a step forward in my career in football and where better to start than at the club which gave me my first break all those years ago?

I happen to think that man-management is one of my strengths. After all, I have worked with some of this country's most distinguished and successful managers during my career and I have learned something from all of them.

And if you don't think I am capable of raising my voice, just ask my family!

Back where it all began, although Chester were now playing at the Deva Stadium

Liverpool Masters

I've always enjoyed taking part in the Masters tournaments. It's getting a little bit tougher for us older guys though, coming up against players who are still fully fit.

A lot of the teams are getting younger and younger now. Some teams like Leicester and Rangers have included lads in recent years who are still playing for clubs. That says a lot. But it's all about playing for the fans.

Liverpool FC
CLUB AMBASSADOR

It was a pleasure to play for Liverpool Football Club for 15 seasons and I'm delighted to now be working in my current role as a global ambassador.

Because of all the experience I gained with the club and my passion for football, it feels like a natural fit for me. I enjoy it and I'm often asked what kind of things I have to do as part of the job. Let me explain.

I'm heavily involved in the club's International Football Academies. That means I travel around the world to oversee how they are run in different countries and to monitor the development of young players.

I have to say, though, that my job isn't just about Liverpool finding the next Steven Gerrard, Jamie Carragher or Raheem Sterling, although obviously that would be great.

Bringing Liverpool FC to other countries and teaching kids around the world the same

EUROPEAN UNION
UNITED KINGDOM OF
GREAT BRITAIN
AND NORTHERN IRELAND

Bobby Charlton and me at the Manchester United v Liverpool game in 2013

methods that are used on the training ground at Melwood are very much two of my main targets.

Basically, my role is to be there when there is an opening of an academy or soccer school. I act as a representative for Liverpool FC.

I am there to deal with all the press requirements that are needed and also to talk about how great the club is, has been in the past and how we're looking forward to the future as well.

We're trying to bring the brand of Liverpool Football Club to the younger generation.

We've got to try and give them that little bit extra to show how special Liverpool Football Club is.

It is a special club – and my role is to talk about that. We are looking for talent, but we are also looking to boost the brand of Liverpool FC around the world.

On the technical side of things, the job involves me developing the soccer schools programme by ensuring things are done in the Liverpool way. »

There are specifics I look at and that includes the coaching the kids are getting. I look at what goes on in first team training at Melwood down to the Academy at Kirkby and then ensure the soccer school franchises are being run in the Liverpool way.

It's no good going to Hong Kong doing one thing and then going to Dubai and doing something completely different.

Everyone has to be working in the same way worldwide and it's down to me to be saying 'this is how Liverpool train, this is what you need to do'.

Obviously only a very small number of youngsters who visit a Liverpool soccer school will go on to play for the club, so there is a big focus on the kids who attend having fun and enjoying themselves as well as explaining the importance of keeping fit and healthy.

It's always great to meet up with old team-mates at the game

The kids are also learning basic talking skills for when they go into jobs later in life.

A lot of the children, when they come to the schools, are very shy and it's up to the coaches and ourselves to try and help them in the right way to get them feeling more confident.

We encourage them to try things and if it doesn't come off, then to try and try again.

You've got to have a positive attitude. If you have a negative one and tell someone 'that was no good', I think they just get down. You have to give them confidence so when they go on to work later in life, they can give confidence to other people as well.

At Liverpool, we are one big family club and that's the way we have to look at it. We've always been known as a family club and we share everything we have. Now we're sharing the football skills they have at the Academy.

People may say I'm biased, but I think Liverpool Football Club is the best club in the world and we've got to give these kids the best facilities and the best coaching that we've got.

THIS IS THE
LIVERPOOL FOOTBALL CLUB
ACADEMY

Walk on, with hope

he thing about a scrapbook is that you could carry on adding to it forever.

For me, I wanted this scrapbook to be mainly about my playing career, but that's not to say my life in football is over. Far from it.

I was very lucky to have had such a good footballing career. The support I was given from fans throughout the world, whether I was playing for Chester, Liverpool, Juventus, Leeds, Newcastle, Wrexham or Wales – was fantastic and I'd like to thank you all for that.

I see myself as a supporter now. A Liverpool and Wales supporter.

I love going to the matches, I love to see my teams doing well and I desperately want to see Liverpool win the league or Wales qualify for a major summer tournament.

I've gone from a player with Liverpool to a club ambassador and I have to say that the welcome I receive from Liverpool supporters, many who never saw me play, wherever I travel to, is phenomenal.

The internet and social media have made the world a lot smaller, but Liverpool Football Club has a massive support all over the world, fans who are hugely passionate for the club.

I want to do everything I can as an ambassador to promote the name of Liverpool Football Club and protect our reputation as one of the greatest clubs in the world. Hopefully we will be successful again on the pitch, but you simply cannot buy history or tradition – something I am proud to have been part of at Anfield.

So may I thank each and everyone of you for reading my scrapbook.

I hope you've enjoyed this trip down memory lane as much as I enjoyed putting it together. And, for Liverpool and Wales supporters, I hope there are many more great memories to come.

Ian Rush

NOW TRY OUT MY
DIGITAL SCRAPPBOOK

BUY THE APP AND EXPERIENCE RUSHIE'S AMAZING COLLECTION OF MEMORABILIA COME TO LIFE!

You've read the book, now download the groundbreaking new app.

The Ian Rush Digital ScrAppbook is an exciting new creation that allows you to get even closer to the Anfield legend's personal collection of memorabilia.

Just imagine taking your old scrapbook down from the attic, blowing off the cobwebs and bringing it to life in a magical, dynamic, interactive format for the iPad, iPhone, Android tablet and smartphones. That is what a Digital ScrAppbook does.

The Ian Rush Digital ScrAppbook features personal video and audio of Rushie talking you through his favourite belongings.

It also allows you the experience of touching the medals to bring the stories behind them to life.

You can even rotate his football boots 360° to look at them up close, and flick through exclusive and unseen images from his photo albums.

Ian Rush Scrappbook
DOWNLOAD NOW!

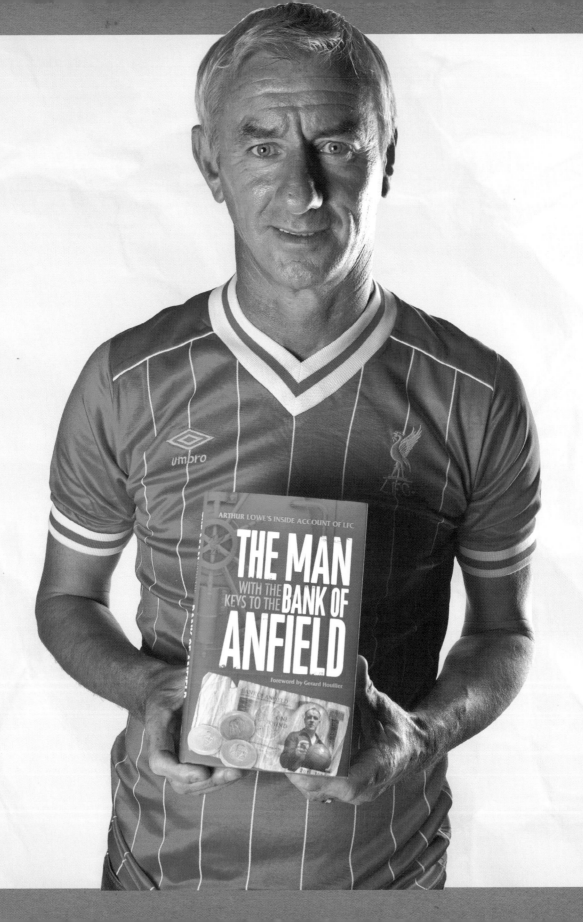

Other Sport Media Books

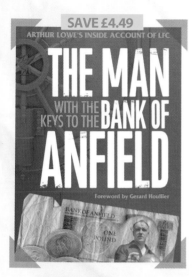
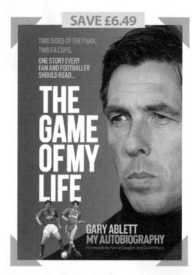

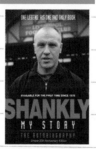

Ian Rush

My SCRAPBOOK

Sport Media S

A Trinity Mirror Business